W9-AHE-925

THE EMPLOYEE ANSWERBOOK™

Practical Answers to the Top 250 Questions Every Employee Has

— DIANA BRODMAN SUMMERS, ATTORNEY AT LAW —

SPHINX® PUBLISHING
AN IMPRINT OF SOURCEBOOKS, INC.®
NAPERVILLE, ILLINOIS
www.SphinxLegal.com

First Edition: 2009

Published by: **Sphinx® Publishing, An Imprint of Sourcebooks, Inc.®**
Naperville Office
P.O. Box 4410
Naperville, Illinois 60567-4410
(630) 961-3900
Fax: 630-961-2168
www.sourcebooks.com
www.SphinxLegal.com

This publication is designed to provide accurate and authoritative information in regard to the subject matter covered. It is sold with the understanding that the publisher is not engaged in rendering legal, accounting, or other professional service. If legal advice or other expert assistance is required, the services of a competent professional person should be sought.

From a Declaration of Principles Jointly Adopted by a Committee of the American Bar Association and a Committee of Publishers and Associations

This product is not a substitute for legal advice.

Disclaimer required by Texas statutes.

Library of Congress Cataloging-in-Publication Data

Summers, Diana Brodman.
  The employee answer book : practical answers to the top 250 questions every employee has / by Diana Brodman Summers.
     p. cm.
  Includes bibliographical references and index.
  1. Employee rights--United States--Miscellanea. 2. Labor contract--United States--Miscellanea.
  3. Labor laws and legislation--United States--Miscellanea. I. Title.
  KF3455.S86 2009
  344.7301--dc22
                              2009002333

Printed and bound in the United States of America.

VP — 10 9 8 7 6 5 4 3 2 1

Contents

Introduction

The rights of employees have always been an important issue to me from my very first job when I saw discrimination firsthand, into my law practice. As many of my former employers will tell you, even before becoming a licensed attorney, I would eagerly go to bat for any co-worker who I thought was being treated unfairly by the bosses. It is with that thirst for fairness and equality at work that I arrived at the point of being an employment attorney.

I find employment law to be a very interesting field because of the quirkiness of the laws. Employment laws in most states are very pro-employer. While it stands to reason that they would be—because the employer has the money to pay the lobbyists—this tends to defeat the goal of the law, which is to protect those who are unable to protect themselves.

Another quirk in some employment laws is a disregard for the principles of fairness. Many federal and state statues get bogged down in the proper form to be used, deadlines to meet, and the minutia of process, rather than the simple humanity of helping someone. We spend the majority of each day at work, more time than most of us spend with our family. During the time we are at work, we may be bombarded with bosses who are bullies, psychopaths, or just incompetent. We do this every day, week after week, year after year, with few if any vacations. Yet, most of us do not know where to look to find out what, if any, our legal protections are. That is what this book is about, providing the reader not only with information but also with places to find more information in the future.

One of the many goals of my law practice has been to provide information to the public about employment law. I believe that if the employee is armed with the tool of knowledge, he or she will be much more effective in dealing with an employer when a problem arises instead of waiting until that problem gets out of hand and requires legal assistance. To that end I provide free information and links on my website at: **www.lawyer4employees.com**. My firm also invites potential clients to call in for a free phone consultation.

This book is a compendium of the most commonly asked questions I have received while in practice at my law firm. It is meant to give an employee answers and solutions to the most commonly asked questions and situations that an employee will encounter. It is not a totally comprehensive study of employment law—that would take several books to cover and would be full of issues that an employee would probably never encounter. I hope it will answer some of your questions.

To my readers, keep sending me your questions. You may find those questions in future books. In the meantime, if you cannot find an answer to your questions in this book, visit the websites I have included in the back of this book.

How to Use This Book

This book is divided into several sections. We first begin with the basics of employment law in Section I. We look at the employee from the legal sense in Chapter 1. In Chapter 2, we look at a separate group of employees—those who work for the government. Chapter 3 gives the reader an overview of the federal laws that protect employees, information on the federal and state agencies that handle employee complaints, where to find laws in your state, and how all the different government and court agencies work together. At the end of this section, in Chapter 4, we discuss employment attorneys.

Section II goes into detail about the employee-employer relationship. Beginning at the hiring process in Chapter 5, we discuss how employers can violate the law even before hiring a person and how things employees write on job applications can get them fired years later. Chapter 6 answers the most common questions about what your employer can and cannot do. Finally, in Chapter 7 we take on a new issue in employment law—bullying. Having a bully in the workplace is an issue that, although going on since the beginning of time, is just starting to be addressed by both lawmakers and health care professionals.

Section III discusses violations of current employment laws. We begin in Chapter 8 with discrimination. In this chapter we look at the current U.S. Equal Employment Opportunity Commission (EEOC) discrimination bases, what the employee needs to prove to win in a discrimination case, and what pitfalls each type of discrimination has in a legal complaint. Chapter 9 describes several nondiscrimination employment laws that govern employees. We also include issues for returning military personnel.

Section IV is all about getting relief for the employee. Chapter 10 goes step by step through how to file complaints with the top four employee-protection agencies in the United States. In Chapter 11 we discuss taking a case to trial—the problems, the costs, and what an employee can ask the court for. Chapter 12 explores the issue of obtaining unemployment benefits. Finally, we end this section in Chapters 13 and 14 with discussions of workers' compensation and the Family and Medical Leave Act (FMLA).

Section V is all about legal agreements between the employer and employee, and how to reach these agreements. We begin with Chapter 15 with a discussion of the very common noncompete agreement. In Chapter 16 we explain both settlement and severance agreements, including what the employee needs to look for in both.

Finally, Chapter 17 goes over the mediation, arbitration, and nego-tiation that potentially go into arriving at a fair agreement.

Section VI is about looking to the future. In Chapter 18 we provide hints on staying employed and how to fight with your employer without being terminated. In the final chapter, we look at where employment law is heading.

When reading this book, please keep a few important things in mind:

- Each state has its own set of laws that affect the employer-employee relationship.

- The best way to find your state's specific laws is by visiting your state's website.

- You can do your own research on local and federal laws, but you may find it much easier to speak with a local employment attorney who can review your specific case as it relates to the relevant laws.

- It is impossible for one book to contain all the variations that affect employees in the United States.

Disclaimer: Nothing in this book implies or should be construed as creating an attorney-client relationship between the reader and the author, Sourcebooks, or any agent thereof.

THEY CAN'T DO THAT—THE TWENTY-FIVE MYTHS OF EMPLOYMENT LAW

- Myth 1: A court can immediately stop my employer from terminating me.
- Myth 2: Employers are legally required to have a legitimate or valid reason for any termination.
- Myth 3: By law, a termination is not effective until the employer gives the employee written notice of termination.
- Myth 4: The employer must follow all the steps of progressive discipline that are listed in the employee handbook.
- Myth 5: My employer/manager/boss cannot legally give friends or relatives jobs or promote them over the current employees.
- Myth 6: An employee should never agree to a separation or severance agreement because he or she can get more money than is offered by suing the employer.
- Myth 7: An employee cannot get unemployment benefits if he or she is getting severance from the employer.
- Myth 8: When there are layoffs or downsizing, employees who have been with the employer the longest will not be terminated until after all newer employees are let go.
- Myth 9: An employee can always get unemployment benefits from the state, even if he or she quit his or her job.
- Myth 10: If an employee files a discrimination complaint against the employer with the EEOC or the state's human rights office, that agency will get the employee a large financial settlement.
- Myth 11: Employers are so afraid that employees will sue them for discrimination that they automatically offer a huge settlement, especially if a lawyer is involved.
- Myth 12: All types of discrimination in the workplace are considered illegal.
- Myth 13: An employee can have his or her boss/supervisor/employer arrested for discrimination.

- Myth 14: Quitting a job is the best way to fight workplace discrimination.
- Myth 15: An employee cannot be terminated merely due to an accusation of sexual harassment—"he said/she said"—without actual evidence.
- Myth 16: An employer cannot change the duties of a particular job, the hours of work, or the actual location of the job.
- Myth 17: If an employee was fired for cause, he or she cannot get unemployment benefits.
- Myth 18: An employer must offer health care insurance to all employees.
- Myth 19: An employer cannot terminate an employee who is out sick but has a doctor's note.
- Myth 20: An employer cannot legally say negative things about previous employees.
- Myth 21: An employee does not need to include all past jobs on a job application.
- Myth 22: The employee's union must immediately get the employee's job back without any pay loss.
- Myth 23: If an employee files a grievance regarding discrimination with the union, the employee does not need to file a discrimination complaint with the EEOC or the state's human rights office.
- Myth 24: The employee's union will handle a discrimination grievance quickly so that the employee can still file a complaint with the EEOC or state's human rights office.
- Myth 25: I do so much more work than any other employee. I am responsible for so many things that are necessary for the company to run successfully that it really cannot get along without me. My employer knows how valuable I am, and if I'm fired, the company will take a serious hit and may fold. I am so good at what I do and so important to this company that it cannot continue without me, and it will never terminate me!

A myth is something that a lot of people believe is true or should be true but really is false. Employment law is especially complex and confusing, so it is ripe for these types of beliefs. The problem comes when an employee relies on a myth or the word of an ill-informed friend when making crucial decisions about his or her employment.

In my practice of helping employees, I have found several common myths that employees believe can hurt them when dealing with an employer.

The following are the top twenty-five general myths that most people believe are true about employment law. Most of these myths deal with issues of common fairness and doing the right thing for the workers.

Please note that while generally all these are myths and do not exist, in some states the elected officials—in order to achieve fairness—have turned one or more of these myths into actual law. Before you act, do your homework. Use the information provided in the appendices at the back of this book to research your state's laws.

Myth 1: A court can immediately stop my employer from terminating me.

The truth is that in employment law, unlike in criminal law, there are no emergency motions or quick fixes that can prevent an employer from terminating an employee. If the employee is a member of a union that has a contract with the employer, the employee may be able to get the union to fight against termination quicker than a non-union employee could. There is no such thing in employment law as a *temporary restraining order* (TRO) that can keep the employer from terminating the employee.

Myth 2: Employers are legally required to have a legitimate or valid reason for any termination.

If the employee is considered *at will*—that is, not under a union contract or an employment contract—the employer does not need any reason for termination. The exception to this is an employer who terminates an employee due to reasons of specific discrimination. Then the employer is subject to a legal complaint, and in the legal proceeding the employer will be required to provide the court with a nondiscriminatory reason for the termination.

Myth 3: By law, a termination is not effective until the employer gives the employee written notice of termination.

Without a union or other contract, the employer is under no legal obligation to inform the employee of the reasons for the termination. At will employees can be terminated either verbally or in writing. There is no legal requirement for a written notice of termination. Again, in a discrimination complaint the employer may want to have such a document as evidence to prove that the reasons for the termination were not discriminatory.

Myth 4: The employer must follow all the steps of progressive discipline that are listed in the employee handbook.

An at will employee can be legally terminated without following any of the steps of progressive discipline found in the employee handbook or the policies in the employer's policy book. This is a source of much confusion, especially since the employee is required to follow the rules listed in the employee handbook or the employer can accuse the employee of a serious rule violation. Unfortunately the law does not require that the employer follow its own rules. However, if the employee files a discrimination complaint, the employer may be required to explain why it ignored its own rules and policies. Even in an action to obtain unemployment benefits, an employer that does not follow its own rules and policies is considered suspect as to the true reason for the termination. Union contracts and other types of employment contracts usually require certain steps of progressive discipline, except for what are considered to be serious violations.

Myth 5: My employer/manager/boss cannot legally give friends or relatives jobs or promote them over the current employees.

As long as the better treatment is not due to discrimination and is not contrary to a union or employment contract, the employer is free to hire or promote friends and relatives. Currently, no state makes it against the law to practice *nepotism*—providing jobs for family members—in the workplace. If an employee files a discrimination complaint against this employer, the hiring or promotion will probably be investigated to see if it violated the current discrimination laws.

Myth 6: An employee should never agree to a separation or severance agreement because he or she can get more money than is offered by suing the employer.

Each separation or severance agreement should be reviewed by a local employment attorney to make sure that all terms conform to the current law and that the employee is aware of the rights that he or she is giving up. In the majority of cases, taking an employer to court will not necessarily provide the employee with a larger windfall, unless the actions of the employer were so egregious that a court will find for the employee. Please remember that suing an employer does not always mean that the employee will end up with more money, especially after court costs and legal fees are deducted from the award. Again, the best bet is to have a local attorney review the agreement, advise the employee, and possibly enter into negotiations for additional benefits.

Myth 7: An employee cannot get unemployment benefits if he or she is getting severance from the employer.

Absent a clause in the severance agreement that prohibits the employee from obtaining unemployment benefits, a worker can get unemployment benefits even with a severance agreement. The employee must be totally off the company payroll before applying for unemployment benefits. In some cases the employer will pay the severance to the employee out of the payroll system. That may mean that the employee continues to get normal paychecks for a period of time until the severance amount is paid. In these instances the employer may then retain the employee as still employed in an *inactive status*. Many times the employer will do this while assisting the employee to find a new job through an outplacement association. That will delay unemployment benefits until the severance is paid in full. In the majority of cases the employee is provided with a check for the full amount of severance on the date of separation from the employer and can apply for unemployment immediately following.

Myth 8: When there are layoffs or downsizing, employees who have been with the employer the longest will not be terminated until after all newer employees are let go.

The practice of rewarding long-term employees who have worked for the employer for a longer period of time is just not followed in today's economy, unless it is specified in a union or employment contract. In most downsizings, where the goal is to reduce the employer's expenses, the easiest way is to reduce expenses is to get rid of the long-term employees, who often have the largest salaries. The employer is not legally required to provide to long-term employees any loyalty or any benefits based on seniority.

Myth 9: An employee can always get unemployment benefits from the state, even if he or she quit his or her job.

This is blatantly false. The majority of states will only provide benefits if the employee quit under certain circumstances. These circumstances are generally if the employee quits on direct orders from a health care professional or if the employee has reported sexual harassment to the employer and the employer refuses to take steps to make the workplace free of such harassment. Your state may have additional requirements. If the employee has been terminated, the employer may fight against the employee getting unemployment benefits. The rules for getting these benefits are further discussed in Chapter 12. State law governs the requirements for getting unemployment benefits.

Myth 10: If an employee files a discrimination complaint against the employer with the EEOC or the state's human rights office, that agency will get the employee a large financial settlement.

Neither the *U.S. Equal Employment Opportunity Commission* (EEOC) nor a state's human rights office can force the employer into providing any type of financial settlement. While both of these agencies will work very hard to get the employee some financial relief, that relief is usually limited to a *reimbursement*—an amount close to what the employee has lost. The employee may decide to go after the employer for additional funds by taking the discrimination complaint to the next level and eventually into a court of law.

Myth 11: Employers are so afraid that employees will sue them for discrimination that they automatically offer a huge settlement, especially if a lawyer is involved.

For a long time this was the rule, and still may be in some pockets of the country. However, in most of the United States, the employer has no fear because it will hire a larger law firm to represent it and wait the employee out, or make the employee pursue the complaint through several time-consuming and expensive trials. It is rare for an employer to offer any settlement before going into a legal proceeding.

Myth 12: All types of discrimination in the workplace are considered illegal.

Unfortunately this is still not true. Illegal discrimination or discrimination bases are determined by federal and state laws. Currently some discrimination, like that against obesity, is not against the law. See Chapter 8 on discrimination for more detailed information.

Myth 13: An employee can have his or her boss/ supervisor/employer arrested for discrimination.

Acts of discrimination in the workplace are not considered violations of the criminal code and cannot result in an arrest. However, an employee who is physically assaulted in the workplace by an employer can file criminal charges against that person with the proper authorities.

Myth 14: Quitting a job is the best way to fight workplace discrimination.

The best way to fight workplace discrimination is to report the discrimination to the human resources department, and then allow the employer a period of time to eliminate the discrimination. If the discrimination continues or if the employer refuses to address the behavior, then the employee should consult a local attorney to see what rights he or she has in filing a complaint with the federal or state agency that enforces the laws on discrimination. In real life, employers rarely listen to the complaints of an employee who makes these accusations at the time he or she quits. Once the employee has turned in his or her notice, most human resources departments consider that person to be an unreliable source, someone who is disgruntled and is out for revenge. This is true even when the employee provides written evidence of the discrimination along with his or her notice to quit. In addition, an employee who quits may have difficulty obtaining unemployment benefits.

Myth 15: An employee cannot be terminated merely due to an accusation of sexual harassment—"he said/she said"—without actual evidence.

When an employee files a sexual harassment charge with the employer, the employer, by law, must investigate that charge—even charges that appear to be without any merit. Many employers take these types of accusations very seriously and have a policy of terminating those accused of sexual harassment, even without making a determination that this employee was guilty of anything. The issues of getting due process or being innocent until proven guilty beyond a reasonable doubt are concepts within the legal system—they are not requirements private employers must abide by. Neither federal nor state laws protect a person who is accused of sexual harassment in the workplace because what the harassed may perceive as sexual harassment is subjective, and because the legislators consider sexual harassment to be a very serious charge. Without a union or employment contract, an at will employee can be terminated even when the termination is unfair.

Myth 16: An employer cannot change the duties of a particular job, the hours of work, or the actual location of the job.

As long as these issues are not covered in a union or employment contract, or the changes are not made because of discrimination, the employer can make any or all of these changes, and the employee has no recourse. The changes cannot be due to discrimination or to punish a certain class of workers.

In today's tight economy it is common to require employees to pick up the tasks that were previously assigned to employees who have since been laid off. For economic reasons the employer may also change the hours of work or eliminate an entire shift. Due to rental costs or economic consolidations, employers may relocate entire workplaces of certain departments. Each one of these actions, if not done to discriminate against a protected class of employees, is legal, even if it means that some employees are out of work.

Myth 17: If an employee was fired for cause, he or she cannot get unemployment benefits.

While this is not necessarily true, it really depends on the wording of the state laws which govern distribution of unemployment benefits. In most states an employee who was fired for cause must also have committed *legal misconduct* in order to be prevented from receiving unemployment benefits. While each state defines *legal misconduct*, it generally involves the employer having a rule that the employee was warned not to break and the employee deliberately violating that rule. A local employment law attorney who has experience with unemployment benefit appeals is the best person to determine if your case qualifies.

Myth 18: An employer must offer health care insurance to all employees.

Unfortunately, there is currently no federal law that requires an employer to provide health insurance for employees. Some states are exploring this requirement for all in-state employers, and by the time you read this book, those laws may have already passed in some states. The country is currently in a health care crisis due to increases in the cost of health care. Employers that have always picked up the health care premiums for all employees may be having problems paying the increased costs. As a result, employees are being required to pay more or all of the health care insurance premiums. Many employers are also trying to reduce their health care costs by creating incentives for healthy lifestyle changes and penalties for known unhealthy behavior. Finally, some employers are only offering health care insurance to certain groups of employees or not offering it at all.

Myth 19: An employer cannot terminate an employee who is out sick but has a doctor's note.

Many employers strictly limit the number of absences that an employee is allowed, no matter what the reason is. Employers that require a doctor's note for an illness are usually doing so to make sure that sick days are used for legitimate illnesses. There are some circumstances where a sick employee does have some protection from termination—in the area of disabilities and workers compensation injuries, which will be discussed later. However, a doctor's note does not offer any protection from termination. Also, employees who are terminated for excessive absenteeism may have problems obtaining unemployment benefits.

Myth 20: An employer cannot legally say negative things about previous employees.

Whether or not an employer can say negative things about previous employees depends on the state law of the employer. In the majority of states an employer cannot provide a negative reference about a previous employee. However, some states have discarded that rule. If a person thinks he or she may get a poor reference from a particular boss or manager, it is best to only provide the phone number of the human resources department to any potential employers and provide the potential employer with contact numbers of other people who will provide a good reference.

Myth 21: An employee does not need to include all past jobs on a job application.

The majority of employers do a professional background check as part of the hiring process and will see every job a person has had. For most employers, not including all past jobs on a job application is considered lying or falsifying the application. Once you are hired, that false information is provided to the employer, and it will sit in your employee file to be used by any future manager/supervisor who wants to make a case to terminate you. It is always best to be 100% truthful on any job application.

Myth 22: The employee's union must immediately get the employee's job back without any pay loss.

The actual limits on what a union can do for a member is spelled out in the union contract. If a union employee is terminated for a serious offense, the union may be powerless to get the employee returned to work. Unions are usually not eager to represent an employee who has been terminated for a valid cause because the union officers must walk a fine line between representing their members and destroying their relationship with an employer.

Myth 23: If an employee files a grievance regarding discrimination with the union, the employee does not need to file a discrimination complaint with the EEOC or the state's human rights office.

A union grievance does not take the place of a formal discrimination complaint filed with the EEOC or the state's human rights office. In a large majority of cases, the union will resolve the grievance on behalf of the employee. However, there are instances where the union cannot stop the discrimination, and it takes a federal or state agency to protect the employee.

Myth 24: The employee's union will handle a discrimination grievance quickly so that the employee can still file a complaint with the EEOC or state's human rights office.

Unfortunately it is not unusual for a union to take so long in handling a discrimination grievance that the employee loses his or her right to file a discrimination complaint with the EEOC or state's human rights office. The employee must be aware that both the EEOC and state's human rights offices have time limits on filing such complaints. It is up to the employee to make sure that his or her complaint is filed within the time limit; otherwise, the complaint will be turned away. For some unions that do not want to anger the employers, stalling on a discrimination grievance until beyond the time limit for filing with the EEOC or state's human rights office is commonplace.

Finally...the most common myth that all employees believe at one time in their career:

Myth 25: I do so much more work than any other employee. I am responsible for so many things that are necessary for the company to run successfully that it really cannot get along without me. My employer knows how valuable I am, and if I'm fired, the company will take a serious hit and may fold. I am so good at what I do and so important to this company that it cannot continue without me, and it will never terminate me!

We have all felt this way at one time in our career. We have all done things or said things at work that defy logic because we know "they will not fire me." If you get nothing else from this book, please believe that every employee can be replaced. The legal protection for employees is thin and can be easily overthrown by an employer with deep pockets that is willing to spend large sums on attorneys. Unless you own your own company, you are a vulnerable employee, even if you are also a valuable employee.

Now that you have read the most common myths, let's go into detail about employment law so that you will have the tools to protect yourself in the workplace.

Section I:
Employment Law Basics

This section discusses some of the basic concepts of employment law. Chapters 1 and 2 discuss what an employee is and how certain types of employees have more protection under the law than others. Chapter 3 is a very brief overview of the federal laws that protect employees and how to apply them. Finally, Chapter 4 discusses employment attorneys and how they can be of great assistance to an employee who is going up against his or her employer and the employer's team of attorneys.

Chapter 1

THE EMPLOYEE

- What are the different types of workers?
- What is an at will employee?
- What does being an at will employee mean to workers?
- What is an employment contract?
- What exactly is an independent contractor, and how do I know if I am one?
- I work through a temporary agency. Am I an independent contractor? I am a computer consultant, but I get my jobs through a computer manufacturer. Am I an independent contractor?
- How do employment contracts protect the employee?
- What rights does an independent contractor have in the workplace?
- What should you do if your employer does not follow your employment contract?
- What protections does a union contract give an employee?
- How can a union employee be sure the union is representing him or her in a discrimination complaint?
- What should you do if your union is not adequately representing you?
- How does an employee deal with the human resources department when he or she has a complaint?
- What steps does an employer need to follow to fire an at will employee?
- What happens if my employer goes bankrupt?
- Will I get paid for my accrued sick days if I am fired?
- How much notice is my employer required by law to give to terminate someone?
- How much notice must I give to quit?
- Does the law require that an employer provide an employee with a reason for termination?

What are the different types of workers?

For employment law purposes, employees are divided into those who are considered *at will* and those employees who are covered under a written contract, such as union members and independent contractors.

What is an at will employee?

The majority of employees in the United States are *at will employees*—those who are not covered by a written contract of employment.

What does being an at will employee mean to workers?

At will employees can be terminated for any reason without notice, except for discrimination, which will be covered in detail in Chapter 8.

Many states call themselves *at will states*, which technically means that state law requires a written union or employment contract as proof for employment that is not considered to be at will. At one time, some states considered the employee manual to be a written contract between the employer and employee. However, this is no longer the case in most jurisdictions, although there are still cases that allege that the specific terms within an employee manual makes it an employment contract.

The at will status allows the employer the legal freedom to make rules and to hire and fire employees as the employer wants, except for cases of discrimination. It is no coincidence that in at will states, the employers have a large and successful lobby with the legislature.

In practical terms, an at will employee has only those rights given to him or her by the state and federal laws that protect employees. An at will employee cannot succeed in a lawsuit for wrongful termination without showing a clear violation of either a state or federal law. As an appellate justice once told me, "Unfair is not always illegal."

> ### <u>Current federal bases of discrimination</u>
>
> - Age (over 40 years old)
> - Color
> - Disability
> - Equal pay
> - National origin
> - Pregnancy
>
> - Sex
> - Sexual harassment
> - Race
> - Religion
> - Retaliation
>
> From the website **www.eeoc.gov**.

What is an employment contract?

What most people refer to as an *employment contract* is a written document between the employer and the employee. The most common is the *union contract* that the union obtains for its members. An employment contract is a document that includes the details such as the type of work, how the work will be judged or delivered, the pay, what happens if either side is not satisfied, and most importantly, how long the contract will last. Many people who work as independent contractors or consultants use employment contracts. That way they are assured of certain details about the work and the amount they will be paid.

What exactly is an independent contractor, and how do I know if I am one?

If you are an independent contractor you will get an IRS form 1099 at the end of the year instead of a W-2. *Independent contractors* usually pay their own taxes, social security, and health care benefits. However, sometimes an employer will pay for certain benefits or fees, such as state fees or health care benefits, as an incentive to keep the independent contractor.

The classic example of an independent contractor is the computer consultant. This person contracts to do certain tasks for a particular company. Many times when a company is purchasing a new computer system, it will call in a consultant to set up the computer and load it with all the software needed.

I work through a temporary agency. Am I an independent contractor? I am a computer consultant, but I get my jobs through a computer manufacturer. Am I an independent contractor?

The true test of being an independent contractor is the IRS 1099 form at the end of the year. Another way to tell is by the name of the company on your paycheck. Most temporary workers are paid by a temp agency—they are employees of the temp agency. The same is true for computer consultants who get their jobs through a computer manufacturer.

That being said, there are many court cases that are brought to answer the question, "Am I an employee?" This usually happens when a worker is in an auto accident or does something that injures another person. Then the employer/temp agency/consulting firm attempts to avoid any liability from the act of the worker. Courts look at the control that the employer has on the worker to determine if he or she is an employee or an independent contractor. The more control the employer has over the worker in terms of what tasks to do, how to do them, when to do them, etc., the more the worker looks like an employee.

How do employment contracts protect the employee?

Employment contracts and union contracts should spell out things like what to do if the employer no longer wants the worker to continue, how much notice is required, and how much severance is required. For independent contractors the contract should detail what happens if the employer does not pay for the work provided, interest rates on balances past due, and other protections that make sure the worker gets the amount of money that was promised.

Employment contracts may also list what is required from the worker. Especially for computer consultants, the contract should detail what computer work is being contracted for, how to know when the computer work is complete, what happens if the computer hardware is defective, and what happens if commercially purchased software is defective. The more details and contingencies that can be put into an employment contract, the better. Because this contract is so important to an independent contractor's future, it is always better to have the contract written—or at least reviewed—by an employment attorney.

What rights does an independent contractor have in the workplace?

An independent contractor has only those rights that are spelled out in the employment contract and certain rights under state and federal laws that are granted specifically for independent contractors. The employment contract should be very detailed and should include specific references to both state and federal laws, so that neither side has questions regarding their rights.

What should you do if your employer does not follow your employment contract?

The remedies for not following the employment contract should clearly be listed in the contract. For an independent contractor or consultant, in addition to the remedies in the contract, the general remedy would be to file a civil suit in a court of law under the theory of a breach of contract. Additionally, for an employee who is employed under a union contract, the employee can file a grievance with the union. If there is no union involved, then depending on the type of violation, the worker may be able to file a complaint with a government agency. A local employment attorney can better advise you on the options available to your for your specific case.

What protections does a union contract give an employee?

Union contracts, like any other employment contract, usually contain details about how to terminate an employee, how pay is structured, when raises are given, and other financial information. The difference here is that a third party, the union, negotiates this legal document for the workers it represents. Many times what the workers want or feel is important is not in these voluminous documents, which are only read by a few union representatives.

A union member should always read his or her union contract to make sure that he or she is getting all the rights and protections in the workplace that are listed in the contract. Union members should lobby their representatives for the benefits that are important to them before contract negotiations between the employer and union even begin.

How can a union employee be sure the union is representing him or her in a discrimination complaint?

Unfortunately, the employee cannot be sure that the union is representing him or her in a discrimination complaint that the employee has brought to the union's attention. In many cases, the union representatives side more with the employer than with the employee when there is an incident of termination or discipline. There is no way around the fact that the union must work daily with the employer and may feel that to go after the employer for just one employee would ruin that working relationship. There is also the issue of union representatives reacting to their personal feelings about a worker instead of enforcing what is in the union contract.

The union member who feels that he or she is being terminated or disciplined due to discrimination should:

1. file a formal grievance with the union; and,

2. consider filing a complaint with the EEOC or the state's human rights agency.

When filing a complaint with the EEOC or state's human rights agency, the employee must make sure that he or she follows the strict time limits imposed by these agencies. The union member may want to get the assistance of a local employment law attorney to advise him or her on how to handle making multiple complaints at the same time.

It is not unusual for a union representative to act slowly on a resolution of a formal grievance until the time has passed for the employee to file a complaint with the EEOC or the state's human rights agency, which is usually a maximum of 180 days. The union representative may want to give the company an opportunity to settle things without the expense of litigation, the union representative may not be able to get the company to talk about the grievance, or in the worst case scenario, the union representative is wasting time on purpose so that the employee has no other recourse but to accept whatever settlement the union can get him or her. Either way, it is up to the worker to make sure that he or she files any complaints for discrimination before the time runs out. See Chapter 10 for more detailed information on this.

What should you do if your union is not adequately representing you?

Poor representation from a union is now becoming a very common complaint. On one side, there are union representatives who have built a good working relationship with an employer—a relationship that has helped the union get more benefits or extra incentives. On the other side, there is a lone employee with a grievance against the employer, whom the union does not seem to be fighting to protect.

The union employee needs to protect him- or herself from this occurring by documenting all grievances filed with the union, documenting problems with the employer, and keeping very good records of all issues the employee has had with the union refusing to represent him or her against the employer. In addition, union employees should not expect any more assistance from their union than what is explicitly listed in the union contract.

If the union employee finds that he or she is in this situation, he or she can contact a local employment law attorney for further assistance. The other option is to file a complaint against the union for *lack of representation* with the National Labor Relations Board (NLRB). See Chapter 10 for more information on this.

How does an employee deal with the human resources department when he or she has a complaint?

The first word of caution is to remember that the human resources department works for the employer's best interests, not the best interests of the employee. While the human resources department might tell you that it will take care of you, proceed with caution. The primary purpose of any human resources department is to make sure that the employer does everything in accordance with the current state and federal laws and avoids litigation. That is all you can legally expect from your human resources department. In a courtroom or at a legal hearing, the human resources department will always side with the employer over you.

Despite that, the employee must report any instances of discrimination, harassment, or other illegal activity to the human resource department. It is important that these issues be reported in writing and that the employee keeps a copy that is dated when the incident was reported. This will protect the employee. In court cases it is not unusual for employers to swear that they knew nothing of the discrimination and had they known they would have fixed the problem. Many employees' cases are lost because of their lack of documentation.

What steps does an employer need to follow to fire an at will employee?

An at will employee can legally be terminated for anything except discrimination. Legally, the employer does not need to follow its own policies regarding progressive discipline or on how to terminate an employee. However, employers that do not follow their own policies in a termination will look suspicious to the employee's attorney. The fact that policies were not followed can be used in a discrimination complaint as evidence that the employer treated this particular employee differently than other employees. *Different treatment* is part of the proof needed to show discrimination.

For the employer that wishes to terminate an employee, the standard advice is to follow the corporate policies to the letter, document every error that the employee has made in writing, use progressive discipline for those infractions that are considered serious or flagrant, and keep the employee informed throughout the entire process.

On the employee side, when an employee receives a written notice of discipline, a written performance improvement plan, or any other document that negatively comments on the employee's actions or performance, the employee should consider him- or herself on notice that the employer may be considering termination. The employee should react by working toward improving the actions or performance he or she has been cited for. While many times an employee feels personally wronged by such criticism, in order to keep that job, the employee must convey to the employer that he or she is ready and willing to change his or her actions.

What happens if my employer goes bankrupt?

It depends on if the employer is asking for reorganization or is just trying to cancel all outstanding debt. The employee's salary is considered a debt owed by the company. In a reorganization the employee may be asked to work for a lower salary with the promise that past due salary will be paid later. For the employer that shuts its doors and goes into bankruptcy, the employees may stand with the rest of the creditors who are owed money by the employer. Bankruptcy trustees are usually very cognizant about paying employees for the work already performed. Issues of vacation earned and other employee benefits can take some time to resolve. If your employer shuts its doors, immediately apply for unemployment benefits to tide you over until you can obtain another job.

Will I get paid for my accrued sick days if I am fired?

Probably not. Under the laws in the majority of states, employers are not legally required to provide any paid sick days to employees. Therefore, the employee does not legally own the sick days that he or she accrues while employed.

If, however, the employee accrues days off that are not separated by vacation time and sick time, then the time may be considered as accrued time off and fall under the Department of Labor's definition of *vacation time*.

How much notice is my employer required by law to give to terminate someone?

If the employee is covered under a union or employment contract, the amount of notice the employer is required to give the employee should be one of the terms in the contract. For at will employees, however, the employer is not required to provide any notice before termination.

How much notice must I give to quit?

Just as in the previous answer, it depends on whether the employee is covered by a contract. If an employee is about to give notice, he or she must follow the terms of his or her union or employment contract. If there is no contract, then the employee must follow the rules set out by the employer about notice. These rules are usually found in the employee manual.

When leaving a job, the employee should make every effort to leave the job in a professional manner. This means that an employee should provide a certain amount of notice for the employer before leaving the job. In the majority of businesses, two-week notice is considered proper. Some employers ask for more notice due to the type of business. Make sure that you review the section in the employee manual on giving notice before you quit your job.

The major reason an employee should provide notice is to protect his or her business reputation. Many employers consider walking off a job without giving notice to be a major affront to the employer. Although the employee may want to do that to get back at the employer, that type of behavior can only hurt the employee. While many states may limit what a former employer can say about an employee to a potential future employer, sometimes a person's reputation is injured by former co-workers who talk to friends they have outside of the office.

Does the law require that an employer provide an employee with a reason for termination?

Unless the employee is under a union or employment contract that requires a reason for termination, employers are not required to provide a reason to terminate an at will employee. Many times the employee is told why he or she was fired when the employee files for unemployment benefits or when the employee brings a discrimination suit against the employer. And even then the reason that the employer offers may not be the complete truth.

Chapter 2

GOVERNMENT EMPLOYEES

- Are government employees treated differently than employees of private employers?
- How can a government employee find out about his or her options if facing a wrongful termination?
- What laws protect government employees from discrimination?
- What are the usual steps a government employee must take to file a discrimination complaint?
- How is the government employee's attorney paid?
- Is mediation better than litigation?
- Is mediation better than litigation for a government employee?
- What may a government employee ask for as a remedy when filing a discrimination complaint?
- How can I appeal a decision against me?
- What is the Merit Systems Protection Board, and how can I use it?
- What are Equal Employment Opportunity officers, and how do they differ from the investigators in the EEOC?

Are government employees treated differently than employees of private employers?

Yes. In most situations a government employee has more options and avenues to pursue when there is a problem such as being bypassed for a promotion, being discriminated against, or being terminated. This is especially true for employees of the federal government. As stated in the first chapter, an at will employee has very few rights—except for the laws preventing discrimination—if his or her employer wants to terminate his or her job. After a probationary period, government employees are different. They have several options if they are faced with wrongful termination. In our current economy—where employee benefits are becoming fewer and fewer—government employees are in the better position regarding benefits and being treated fairly compared to nongovernment, at will workers.

How can a government employee find out about his or her options if facing a wrongful termination?

A government employee's options depend on the agency, department, or government body that the person works for. There are few generalities that can be listed because people who work for the government—especially for the federal government—are typically governed by the rules and regulations set out for that specific agency or department. The policies and procedures set forth by the specific departments are usually the ones that have to be followed.

Before a government employee decides to file a complaint against an employer or go to court, he or she must do the research to see if there are steps required to initiate an internal grievance. If you are a government employee, do not expect the courts or the U.S. Equal Employment Opportunity Commission (EEOC) to know what the specific internal procedures you need to follow are before you are allowed to file a discrimination complaint. Government offices typically have poor, if any, communication with each other.

A common example is that many government agencies and state offices require that an employee file a formal discrimination complaint, following specific procedures, with that agency's Equal Employment Opportunity (EEO) officer, before going outside of the office. The EEO officer's job is to attempt to resolve the discrimination issue before the complaint is escalated outside of the office and litigation becomes a possibility. Some of the mandatory deadlines for filing internal grievances or complaints can be very short, so it is very important for government employees to learn the specific policies and regulations of their agency.

It is unfortunate when a government employee does not do his or her homework and starts filing a complaint outside of his or her department or hires a private attorney only to discover that he or she neglected to follow the correct procedures and exercise all of his or her options for the case. By exercising all the employee's options and following time requirements, government employees lay a stronger foundation for litigation and winning their case if they end up in court.

I have heard many government employees complain that these regulations are a burden and another challenge for the employee who has already suffered from discrimination. It may be true that in some agencies the regulations can be another hassle for an employee who is having problems at work and that some managers might take advantage of the regulations to make the employee jump through hoops as further punishment. However, this is certainly not the purpose of regulations and procedures. The legitimate purpose is to resolve the employee's problem fairly, quickly, and without external interference. The vast majority of cases are successfully handled in this manner.

What laws protect government employees from discrimination?

Just like most nongovernment employees, government employees are covered by Title VI, the Age Discrimination in Employment Act, and the Equal Pay Act. Those working for the federal government are covered by Sections 501 and 505 of the Rehabilitation Act of 1973, which incorporates the requirements set out in the Americans with Disabilities Act. Most federal agency employees—except those in the FBI, CIA, DIA, NSA, or by direction of the President—are also covered by the Civil Service Reform Act of 1978. The agency, department, or branch of government that an employee works for may have additional regulations that provide protection for the employee. The primary difference between government employees and private sector employees is in the processing of complaints.

Federal government employees should visit **www.opm.gov**, which is the website for the Office of Personnel Management (OPM). Those employed by other government entities may have a similar personnel management or human resources office. Some states have statutes that specifically address government employees and their complaints.

Federal government employees are technically covered by the Civil Service Reform Act of 1978 (CSRA). This law prohibits federal employees from being discriminated against on the basis of race, color, sex, religion, national origin, age, disability, marital status, political affiliation, or conduct that does not adversely affect performance. The OPM has interpreted the prohibition of discrimination based on conduct to include sexual orientation. (See **www. opm.gov/er/address2/guide01.htm**.)

The Office of Special Counsel (OSC) and the Merit Systems Protection Board (MSPB) enforce the CSRA. The OSC defers those bases of discrimination that are covered by the EEOC to the agency involved and their EEO process. There are other areas where the OSC will decide to also address a federal employee's complaint. These areas include discrimination due to marital status, discrimination due to political affiliation, interference with another's promotion or application for government employment, nepotism, whistle-blowing, retaliation, violations of the Freedom of Information Act, or discrimination based on personal conduct that does not affect job performance. (See **www.osc.gov/ppp.htm**.)

What are the usual steps a government employee must take to file a discrimination complaint?

These are the steps a government employee typically must take in order to file a discrimination complaint against the agency or department he or she works for:

1. Contact an EEO counselor at the agency where the discrimination took place within forty-five days of the discriminatory action.

2. Decide between either the EEO counseling or an alternative dispute resolution program if the agency offers one. Counseling must be completed within thirty days, An alternative dispute resolution program must be completed within ninety days.

3. If counseling or the alternative dispute program are not successful, then the employee can file a formal complaint with the agency.

4. The agency is required to conduct an official investigation.

5. If the complaint contains at least one issue that can be appealed to the Merit Systems Protection Board (MSPB), the employee then has the option of sending the case to the MSPB to be processed under the Board's procedures. When an employee

sends a case to the MSPB, the employee has the option of either proceeding to a full trial with witnesses, or he or she can provide the MSPB with all relevant documents along with a legal brief. If you are in this situation, you should consult with an attorney to determine which option is best for your case.

6. For a case that is brought before the MSPB, if the employee does not agree with the decision, he or she can appeal the parts of the decision concerning discrimination to the EEOC. The employee can also take an appeal of the MSPB ruling to the United States Court of Appeals for the Federal Circuit.

7. If the complaint does not contain an MSPB issue, the employee may either request a hearing before an EEOC administrative judge or an immediate final determination from the agency.

8. If the employee does not agree with the final determination from the agency, the employee has thirty days to appeal to the EEOC.

9. If the employee decides to have an EEOC hearing, the administrative judge must issue a decision within 180 days. If the judge finds that the complaint is valid and that there was discrimination, the judge will order the appropriate relief. The agency then has forty days from receiving the order of relief from the judge to comply with the ruling. However, if the agency does not agree with, or refuses to comply with, the order from the EEOC administrative judge, the agency must file an appeal within forty days. On the other hand, if the employee does not agree with the decision of the EEOC administrative judge, the employee must file an appeal within forty days.

How is the government employee's attorney paid?

In most cases, if a government employee hires a private attorney to represent him or her in a discrimination case and the attorney wins the case for the employee, the attorney's fees are usually paid by the losing party—the government. This is especially true if the attorney has represented the employee in formal mediation or in a formal trial.

Is mediation better than litigation?

Mediation means that a neutral party meets with the employee, the employee's attorney, a government representative, and the government representative's attorney in order to come to a fair consensus. Mediation is not supposed to result in an outcome that is favorable to one side, but unfavorable to the other; both sides must compromise. A successful mediation is when both parties come away from the table having given something up and having gotten something in return. In mediation, there is no absolute winner, but the benefit is that the parties no longer have to resort to bringing their case in front of a judge.

When a government employee has followed the steps and procedures in filing a discrimination complaint, there may come a time when the government offers formal mediation to resolve the conflict. This can also occur when the employee's attorney has filed a request for a Merit Systems Protection Board (MSPB) trial, and then also files a formal request with the MSPB for directed mediation. The government employee must go into mediation with the resolve to compromise; mediation is not the place to be insistent on getting entirely your own way.

Is mediation better than litigation for a government employee?

Mediation is certainly less expensive than taking a case to trial. It is also less contentious for an employee who wants to make a career in the government and who will have to return to work with the same people. Mediation does not rely on hurting the other side's feelings or making the other side furious; its basis is compromise.

Because mediation can come very late in the process for a government employee—sometimes years after the complaint was first initiated—many times the employee is out for revenge. If the employee is not willing to compromise, the employee needs to sit down with his or her attorney to examine the costs of a trial and whether or not there is a real possibility of winning the case in court. If there is not, the employee needs to reexamine his or her position on compromising.

What may a government employee ask for as a remedy when filing a discrimination complaint?

There are a handful of available remedies a government employee may ask for, including:

- the positing of a notice to all employees advising them of their rights under the laws EEOC enforces and the right to be free from retaliation for exercising these rights;

- actions that will correct the discrimination complained of going forward;

- nondiscriminatory placement of the employee in the position he or she would have occupied had the discrimination not occurred;

- compensatory damages, such as fees the employee had to pay to attorneys to bring the discrimination complaint;

- back pay and costs for lost benefits; and,

- stopping the specific discriminatory practices complained of.

How can I appeal a decision against me?

As a government employee, you will receive information about appealing the decision throughout the complaint process. Once you begin the formal complaint procedure, you need to read everything sent with the decision and pay special attention to anything mentioning specific deadlines.

It is not unusual for an employee to be required to notify his or her agency or department within a very short period of time—sometimes as little as seven days—if he or she wishes to proceed to the next step of the complaint process.

Appealing a decision is an area where you may want to get the input from an attorney. The attorney can look at the specific details of your case, project costs, and may be able to help you with the appeal. However, keep in mind that as you continue to appeal decisions against you, the end result may be a full trial, which can be costly.

What is the Merit Systems Protection Board, and how can I use it?

The Merit Systems Protection Board (MSPB) is an appellate-level court that hears certain cases on employment issues brought by government employees. An employee needs to receive permission to bring a case before the MSPB. Permission is usually given after several decisions have been made against the employee. Once an employee is given permission to file the case with the MSPB, he or she does so by filling out a very long form.

If you are planning on hiring an attorney for your MSPB appeal, let your attorney fill out the form. For attorneys who routinely handle

MSPB cases, there are issues of trial strategy that may be decided with the responses entered on this form. For example, in a case where there are no witnesses and only a disagreement as to documentation, the attorney may want to submit briefs and paper evidence to the judge, instead of having an actual, expensive, in-person trial.

Make no mistake; the MSPB is a real trial. The difference is that the MSPB appeal goes faster than most trials. In a very short amount of time after filing the completed form with the MSPB, the judge assigned to the case will call several pretrial conferences. Discovery, submission of evidence, and depositions are completed in a much shorter time period than in a civil or criminal trial. It is not unusual for an MSPB trial to begin within a few months of the form being filed.

It is common for the MSPB trial to end with the judge asking each side to submit a final argument brief within thirty to ninety days. After that, the parties will wait several months for a written decision. An MSPB trial is a lot of work for a knowledgeable attorney and probably is not something that should be done by someone without legal assistance.

What are Equal Employment Opportunity officers, and how do they differ from the investigators in the EEOC?

An agency's Equal Employment Opportunity (EEO) officer works in that particular agency and deals with government employees only. An investigator at EEOC can investigate claims from private and government employees. Both of these professionals have to power to require documents, take statements from witnesses, apply laws, and render legal decisions. Although the EEO officer works for the agency, he or she is required to be neutral and to produce a decision that is in line with what the law. That neutrality is also required of all EEOC investigators.

Chapter 3

THE LAW

- Does every state have its own department or agency that handles employee complaints?
- How does someone who is not an attorney know where to take his or her complaint?
- What is a dual filing, and how do I know if I have one? Which agency gets priority?
- Why would I go to the federal agency instead of the state agency?
- What are the actual laws against discrimination?
- How can I find out what the law actually says?

Does every state have its own department or agency that handles employee complaints?

For some types of employee complaints or inquiries there are both state and federal offices. When there are both state and federal offices, the state office enforces only the state laws, while the federal office only enforces the federal laws.

The following are the common issues that employees have and which department or agency handles that issue:

- **Unemployment.** Each state has its own agency that distributes unemployment benefits and its own laws regulating the distribution. Across the country most states have almost identical requirements for an employee to qualify for benefits. The major differences are in how each program is funded. The federal office merely oversees the state offices.

- **Discrimination.** The federal office of the EEOC has an office in each state to allow for the filing of discrimination complaints. The EEOC offices all enforce the same laws and handle investigations in the same manner. Because of this, it is not unusual for an EEOC complaint that is filed at one of the more active offices to be forwarded to another office in a different state to be processed faster.

    The majority of states also have their own discrimination laws that mirror the laws enforced by the EEOC, although many states have additional discrimination bases. State offices are departments of that individual state's government. Some states have complex human rights agencies that contain not only an investigative branch but a trial and an appellate branch within the complex. On the other hand, there are states that merely refer their citizens to the local EEOC office and do not have any additional laws other than what the EEOC enforces.

- **Workers' compensation.** For the issue of workers' compensation each state has its own agency and set of laws. As with unemployment, there is federal oversight for all state offices.

- **Department of Labor.** The Department of Labor (DOL) is a multifunctional, multioffice conglomerate within both state and federal areas. Technically, the Secretary of the Department of Labor is the head of all DOL offices.

The structure of the DOL offices is complex. A state may have several DOL offices. These offices enforce state DOL rules along with some federal regulations. Some state offices have more power and handle more work than others. These state offices may have websites where an employee can download a complaint form and find extensive information.

The federal DOL also enforces federal labor laws and specialty areas such as OSHA. The federal DOL has all of its information available online. Its website is the most complete repository of anything related to the Department of Labor. Its website is **www. dol.gov**. To find your state's DOL office see Appendix B.

How does someone who is not an attorney know where to take his or her complaint?

Each government agency—federal and state—has a website with great information on where you need to take your complaint. For unemployment benefits and workers' compensation issues, you only need to deal with your state office. If you have a discrimination complaint, find your state office and EEOC office. You can look at Appendix A to find your state office, or you can go to the website **www.eeoc.gov**. While there may be some reasons to file with the federal agency instead of the state agency, in most cases an employee's complaint will have a dual filing in both locations.

If you have a complaint that falls under the Department of Labor, things become more confusing. The federal Department of Labor is made up of several other agencies, such as OSHA, so if the complaint falls under that heading, you may need to file with the federal DOL. However, your state's DOL office may be one that handles many different areas of law, so the best idea is to go to that website first for more information. The other option, of course, is to contact an employment attorney who can point you in the right direction.

What is a dual filing, and how do I know if I have one? Which agency gets priority?

Dual filing is usually an issue when dealing with a discrimination complaint, although some Department of Labor issues can be filed with both the state and federal arm of the DOL. The two agencies involved in a discrimination dual filing are the federal EEOC and the state's human rights department. In most states, the form you need to fill out to initiate a discrimination complaint allows you to automatically file in both the state and federal offices. If at all possible, check the box that allows an automatic dual filing.

Sometimes, though, because the EEOC may allow a longer time before actually filing the complaint or because the state has additional laws that cover more situations than the federal laws do, the complaint may only be filed with one agency. You will know that your discrimination case has been filed in both offices because both the EEOC and the state agency will assign the complaint a case number. So your single complaint will get two separate numbers that will be displayed on all correspondence from the agencies to you.

The priority issue is another one of those things that you can decide when you initiate the complaint. For an employment attorney, this decision is strategic, based on how backlogged the agencies are, who will provide voluntary mediation, who will help broker a settlement, or what the attorney wants to do with the case. If the attorney wants the case to end up in federal district court, the EEOC will take priority. If the attorney wants the case to stay in the state courts, the state agency will take priority.

Why would I go to the federal agency instead of the state agency?

Dual filing is usually the best, but sometimes it is better to select one agency over the other. The decision as to whether to file in the state or federal agency is based on a number of factors that need to be evaluated. The following are some of the more important considerations.

- **Time.** Each agency has a specific length of time in which you are allowed to file a complaint. The time starts when the major event occurs—for example, termination or the incident of discrimination—and usually each day is counted (including weekends and holidays). The length of time allowed varies by agency and by state. If you wait too long to file with an agency, you will lose your opportunity to have it hear your complaint. These time limitations are strictly enforced without exception.

- **Law.** The second major consideration is the laws enforced by the agency. In many states, the state discrimination law covers more bases of discrimination than the federal laws. Find the agency whose law covers the type of discrimination you suffered, and file your complaint with that agency.

- **Location.** Some agencies—especially the federal ones—are in charge of regulating multiple states. Your selection of an agency office in which to file your complaint will depend on the office that is assigned to your location.

- **Future.** The selection of where to file may depend on what you intend to do with your complaint. Do you intend to file your complaint with the EEOC and take your case to federal district court? Do you want to keep your complaint local and in the state courts?

- **Knowledge.** This is the realm of the experienced attorney who routinely practice employment law. Attorneys may have experienced long time delays, no mediation, or other issues with one of the agencies and may decide that for your case it is better to file your complaint with either the state or the federal agency because of these issues.

What are the actual laws against discrimination?

The federal government prohibits discrimination for a number of reasons, including age, race, sex, color, religion, and national origin. *The U.S. Equal Employment Opportunity Commission* (EEOC) enforces all of these laws. EEOC also provides oversight and coordination of all federal equal employment opportunity regulations, practices, and policies.

Each state has its own laws about discrimination. The state laws mirror what the federal laws say, and in most states the laws have additional bases for what is considered discrimination. Currently, many states are adding laws to prohibit discrimination due to sexual orientation and discrimination due to being in the military. Remember that the law is always evolving.

The current federal laws prohibiting job discrimination are:

- **Title VII of the Civil Rights Act of 1964** (Title VII), which prohibits employment discrimination based on race, color, religion, sex, or national origin;

- the **Equal Pay Act of 1963** (EPA), which protects men and women who perform substantially equal work in the same establishment from sex-based wage discrimination;

- the **Age Discrimination in Employment Act of 1967** (ADEA), which protects individuals who are 40 years of age or older;

- **Title I and Title V of the Americans with Disabilities Act of 1990** (ADA), which prohibit employment discrimination against qualified individuals with disabilities in the private sector, and in state and local governments;

- **Sections 501 and 505 of the Rehabilitation Act of 1973**, which prohibit discrimination against qualified individuals with disabilities who work in the federal government; and,

- **Civil Rights Act of 1991**, which, among other things, provides monetary damages in cases of intentional employment discrimination.

How can I find out what the law actually says?

The best tool for researching anything legal is the Internet. Not only can you find the entire text of the law, you can see how that law is usually enforced. In Appendix E, you will find a list of websites that will help you in your research.

If you prefer using books for your research, your local library or a law school library may be able to help you. If you are going to file a complaint with a particular agency, that agency may have written information for you and sometimes may have a research center open to the public.

Remember that the law that is actually enforced is not exactly what is written in the statutes. The law is constantly evolving through judges interpreting the statutes. The law—especially employment law—is not black and white. In employment law, whether something is illegal or not depends on the circumstances surrounding each individual case.

Chapter 4

ATTORNEYS WHO CONCENTRATE ON EMPLOYMENT LAW

- Do I need an employment attorney?
- How do I find an attorney who can help me with an employment law question?
- How much do employment attorneys cost?
- I cannot afford an attorney. Can I do the work myself?
- Does that mean that an employee who represents him- or herself in an employment case will always lose?
- What is the difference between a discrimination complaint written by an attorney and one that is written without an attorney?
- I have collected the names of several employment attorneys. What should I do now?
- Why won't my employment attorney go into federal district court?
- Several employment attorneys told me that I do not have a winnable case. What should I do now?
- I filed a complaint on my own and lost. Will an attorney be able to help me now?
- Do all employment issues have time limits?
- Two years ago the company I worked for fired me without any notice because of my race. I didn't do anything right away because I have been sick. Can an attorney help me with my case now?
- About eighteen months ago I was wrongfully terminated from my union job because of my race. I filed a grievance with the union, but they have been putting off a scheduled mediation with the company. Can an attorney help me?

Do I need an employment attorney?

Whether or not you need an attorney depends on you, your situation, and what you want to achieve. There are certain aspects of employment law where it is important for an employee to have legal advice. Some of these situations include:

- an appeal in an unemployment benefits case;

- a workers' compensation complaint; and,

- when there is direct negotiation with the employer.

As in any legal situation, if the other side brings an attorney with him or her, this can indicate an escalation of the legalities of the case, and you should hire an attorney to represent you.

There is also the issue of emotion in litigation, especially when a person has lost his or her job for what may be an unfair reason. It may be extremely difficult for an employee who was just wronged by his or her employer to maintain the negotiation skills needed to work out a settlement. Employment attorneys become the buffer between the employee and the employer when trying to come to a fair settlement.

An attorney will look at the employee's situation with an eye toward the current laws. Employment attorneys ask questions about how the employee was treated, how the termination was handled, and other issues that may uncover legal violations that a person untrained in this type of law would overlook. Keep in mind that in every legal employment issue the employee is under time constraints. If an employee waits too long to decide what to do, the opportunity for filing a legal complaint may be gone forever. Having an employment attorney review your situation and provide advice will at least provide you with your options and help you make a decision as to what steps to take.

How do I find an attorney who can help me with an employment law question?

There are a large number of laws that can potentially affect an employee and most of them are very complex. While in years past an attorney with a general practice could assist an employee with his or her case, employment laws are becoming more complex and require the expertise of an attorney who is an expert in employment law issues.

The first step to finding an employment attorney who can help your case is to ask friends, family, and business acquaintances for a referral. Another way to find an employment attorney is through a local bar association. There are hundreds of bar associations in the United States. Not all states require licensed attorneys to belong to a particular bar association; however, most attorneys are members of at least one country, state, county, city, or practice-type bar association. These associations usually have attorney referral plans to match the public with their members. Because employment law is state-specific, you should look for an attorney who is licensed in your state.

Along with bar associations, you can find attorneys through other organizations that they belong to. The *National Employment Lawyers Association* (**www.nela.org**) has listings of employment attorneys throughout the country. There are also several online associations that match clients and attorneys. There are websites of various association and organizations listed in Appendix E that might be helpful.

Finally, when looking for a lawyer you can always do an Internet search on words like "employment law," "discrimination," "wrongful termination," "termination," "fired," or "unemployment benefits," plus the name of your state. This will bring up a variety of law firms and attorneys' websites. Being able to read about a law firm and the attorney via a professional, legitimate website is a helpful way to determine if this particular attorney or firm can help you.

Occasionally, I will be asked by a potential client about going up against a big company or a company that is the only employer in town. The employee fears that attorneys in that town will be biased in favor of the big company and are concerned about finding someone who can help them. If you find yourself in this position, you should contact a large law firm in one of the bigger cities in your state. More often than not, the actual courtroom or agency office is actually located in that big city, which makes it easy for the attorney to appear in the court and eliminates the concern of any influence from the employer.

What not to do when dealing with an employment attorney

1. **Refuse to pay the bill.** If a client feels that he or she may have problems with money, this is something that should be discussed with the attorney right away. Not paying a lawyer's legitimate bill can cause you to become engaged in litigation against your attorney.

2. **Call the attorney to ask questions and not write down the answers.** Do not call your attorney to discuss your case while driving or while doing anything else. Also, before you call, make sure that your cell phone is sufficiently functional so that your attorney can hear you and that your call will not be dropped.

3. **Tell lawyer jokes to your attorney.** Most attorneys are polite and do not say how offensive they are, but they are offensive.

4. **Begin your first conversation with a lawyer by being belligerent about the legal profession, about how lawyers rip people off, and about how you won't stand for paying one cent more than the case is worth.** This kind of behavior marks you as a potential problem client and may potentially cause more work or more expense on a simple case, or it may be the reason that an attorney will not take your case.

5. **Neglect to identify yourself when you call your attorney.** When you call your attorney, do not expect him or her to be able to identify you by your voice or remember your case if it was a while ago. Tell the attorney your name and a brief sentence reminding the attorney who you are.

6. **Ignore the advice of your attorney.** Even worse is doing something that is specifically against your attorney's advice and then calling the attorney to help you out of your new problem. Not only will you end up with a higher bill because of the extra work, but there are times when the problem cannot be fixed.

7. **Try to out-lawyer your attorney.** With the ease of the Internet, legal research is available to everyone. However, reading the law on the Internet or reading some cases does not make a person a knowledgeable legal expert. It

is okay to ask your attorney why certain things are being done, but it is not okay to insist on including certain legal issues in your case, even when your attorney disagrees.

8. **Demand that your attorney get you the same arrangement that your cousin, your neighbor, or your friend in another state got.** Each case is unique, and it is usually impossible to accurately compare two different cases. Also, you do not know the details of the other cases. If you really want your case to end up like these other people's cases, ask them for the name of their lawyer and see if that lawyer will look at your case.

9. **Ignore your attorney's directions at a hearing.** There is nothing worse than preparing a client on what to say in front of a judge and then have the client refuse to follow that preparation. Every employment attorney has seen cases fall apart because the client decides that he or she wants to make a statement or add commentary that is against the attorney's preparation and can potentially cause the entire case to be lost.

10. **Refuse to settle because you want to hold out for more money.** While employment cases rarely result in huge settlements, many times they do result in a fair financial settlement. If a client refuses to take the settlement, there may not be another chance for more money. Experienced employment attorneys know when the negotiations on a settlement have ended and will advise the client that the offered amount is probably the final offer they will receive.

Sometimes at that point the client becomes greedy and wants to hold out for more, but that may require the client to get into an expensive court battle, which the client may lose.

11. **Lie to your attorney.** Everything you discuss with your attorney is legally held in confidence due to attorney-client privilege. If you are not honest with your attorney, the attorney will be unable to fully assist you in your case. Nothing is more harmful in a hearing than having the employer bring up some evidence—like a document that implicates the client on some action—which the attorney is not aware of. This can destroy the entire case.

How much do employment attorneys cost?

Attorneys vary in what and how they charge. Attorneys can charge an hourly rate, a flat fee for their services, take a percentage of a settlement amount (called a *contingency*), or a combination of these. Many attorneys will ask for a *retainer* (an amount up front), which they will bill against as they begin to work on the case. Once the retainer gets below a certain dollar amount, the client will be required to replenish it.

Many potential clients ask about a lawyer taking a case for no money up front and accepting a contingency fee at the end of the trial if they win. However, this is not very common with employment cases because in every employment case the majority of the work done by the attorney is done up front. An employment attorney spends the most time and money within the first few months when the case is filed in the proper forum, and there is no guarantee that the case will result in a financial settlement.

If you have financial issues, it is best to bring them up when you first speak with your attorney. There are times when an attorney can make certain adjustments—like taking on only a part of a case—in order to keep the bill down.

I cannot afford an attorney. Can I do the work myself?

The old proverb that a "person who represents himself has a fool for a client," still rings true. Unless you are conversant with the current laws and procedures of employment law, you will probably make mistakes. Filing discrimination complaints with the EEOC and with your state's human rights office may seem easy, and in fact these agencies may tell you that you do not need an attorney.

The primary issue is that a person who is not familiar with the legal aspects of discrimination law may misstate or forget to include something in the complaint that will turn out to be of primary importance as the case proceeds through the legal system.

Another thing to remember when representing yourself is that your employer will have at least one attorney. Many documents that the employer must file in a discrimination complaint are required to be created by an attorney. If there is a fact-finding hearing you will be face-to-face with the attorney and your former employer, but you will have no one with you on your side. Also, by not having an attorney represent you, you will be responsible for handling the negotiations to achieve a settlement. Settlements are not easy to obtain, even for attorneys, and require some knowledge of the potential litigation that can result from an employment discrimination complaint.

Does that mean that an employee who represents him- or herself in an employment case will always lose?

Just like there is no guarantee that an attorney can win your employment case, there is no guarantee that you will lose your case without legal help. A lot depends on how legitimate your complaint is and whether the actions of your employer were actually against the law, as opposed to being merely mean or unfair. In a legal complaint it is only the actual law that matters. The attitude of your employer and whether it is willing to take responsibility for mistakes will also play a large part in whether the case will be settled.

What is the difference between a discrimination complaint written by an attorney and one that is written without an attorney?

The easy explanation is that a complaint written by an attorney not only states what the discriminatory act was, but shows how this act meets all the requirements of the law to be illegal discrimination.

For those people who wish to proceed without attorneys, they may meet with an intake person or just fill out forms on their own to be presented to the state or federal agency. The complaint will be taken from the information obtained on the forms. On the other hand, for those with legal representation, the attorney will meet with the client and ask questions about the discrimination, what happened, when it started, who did what, whether the employee reported the incident, and other relevant information. Using current employment laws, the attorney will draft a complaint that shows how the client was discriminated against and how the instances complained of meet every aspect of the law. The attorney will then file the complaint with the state or federal agency. Once an investigator is assigned, the attorney will work with that investigator to fill in missing information, provide evidence, answer questions, and propose a settlement. The attorney may also contact the employer prior to filing the complaint to see if a settlement can be reached.

Also, the fact that a person has gone to the expense of hiring a professional to write the complaint shows that the employee feels that his or her complaint is so serious that he or she is willing to put money on it.

I have collected the names of several employment attorneys. What should I do now?

You may want to find out more about each attorney and see if he or she handles your type of problem before calling him or her about the specific details of your case. You can do this by looking at the online listings for this attorney. Does the attorney or firm have a website? Are they listed in any of the common legal references listed in Appendix E?

Once you are sure that the attorney has experience in the area of law you need help in, call his or her office. Many employment attorneys offer an initial phone conference, sometimes for free. This is because the area of employment law is so big that the attorney needs to find out if he or she can even help you. Most employment attorneys only deal with a tiny piece of the vast arena of employment law, which is good for their clients because they build up expertise in that area, but it means that you will probably need to speak to several attorneys to find one to precisely fit your case. In that initial phone call you will be able to determine if this attorney can assist you. If you cannot speak with the attorney directly, do not hesitate to ask the office staff if that law office handles your type of case.

At an initial telephone screening the attorney will probably ask you a lot of questions about your case. The attorney wants to see if you are within the proper time limits to proceed with the case, if you are in the right area of law, and if the case is something that the attorney can help you with. Most attorneys will explain billing, time limits, and law firm policies. If the attorney can help you, and if you think this is the person you want to represent you, the next step may be a face-to-face meeting, or if time limits are tight, you may be able to do a lot of the work via phone, fax, and email.

Your attorney will probably want to see several documents regarding your employment. Generally, if the client has been terminated or disciplined, the attorney will want a copy of those documents. If the client is having problems obtaining unemployment benefits, the attorney will want copies of all documents from the state office that issues unemployment benefits. You may also be asked for any evidence of discrimination, a list of potential witnesses to that discrimination, copies of performance reviews, or any other documents issued by the employer or agency. For safekeeping it is usually better to provide the attorney a copy of any original document or just fax a copy of the original to the attorney.

Why won't my employment attorney go into federal district court?

If you have filed a complaint with the EEOC, you may get a *right to sue letter*. The letter allows the employee to sue the employer in federal district court. However, the employee will probably have to pay for his or her own attorney since the EEOC will only represent an employee in very rare instances (approximately 0.01% of all the EEOC cases filed in the United States). Not every attorney who files a complaint with the EEOC or participates in EEOC mediations will take a case into the federal district court.

There are a number of reasons for this. Many district courts require that an attorney agree to be available to assist the court in other pro bono appointed cases in order to be allowed to bring any cases before the court. For a small law firm or solo attorney, a time-consuming pro bono appointment can mean a financial disaster for the firm.

Cases that go into the federal district court are very time-consuming for an attorney. Many attorneys have a full case load with appearance at the EEOC and other agencies, without having to put that work on hold to work up a full district court trial.

Sadly, many cases, although completely valid, are impossible to prove in a court. The common case is where a conversation or act of discrimination happened between the employee and employer, without anyone else being present. Without any solid evidence, the case is very difficult to win because it comes down to he said/she said.

It also may be that the attorney feels that the case will only drain the employee of money and time. Contrary to the popular opinion that most attorneys are only out to take a client's money, most attorneys will sit down with a client who has this type of case and explain that the case can go on for years, cost a lot, and result in a decision that is against the employee.

Several employment attorneys told me that I do not have a winnable case. What should I do now?

You can continue to ask employment attorneys to review your case until you find an attorney whose opinion you trust. Employment law is not like criminal law, where a person either has committed a crime or has not. In employment law there are varying shades for actions and very few cases that immediately appear to be winners. Sometimes an attorney who has previously worked on a particular aspect of law, can win a case that looks totally unwinnable to other attorneys.

That being said, there comes a time where an employee may need to put the bad employment experience behind him or her and move on. It is frustrating for the client and the attorney to know the real reason behind the termination but to have no evidence of anything discriminatory or otherwise illegal to bring into court. There are people who will fight their employers on this kind of issue in every imaginable forum because they want what they feel is right. If you are told by several attorneys that you cannot win your case, you may need to thank the attorneys for not letting you run through your remaining finances in a fruitless attempt to get even with an employer that wronged you.

I filed a complaint on my own and lost. Will an attorney be able to help me now?

Unfortunately, if you already lost your case, an attorney will not be able to help you. Each person gets one chance to make a case. Depending on where you filed your case, you may have no rights to appeal to have your case reopened.

Do all employment issues have time limits?

Yes all employment issues have time limits—or statutes of limitation—and the time limits are very strictly followed. Employee complaints filed with any state or federal agency will have very strict time limits. These are especially relevant when filing unemployment claims, workers' compensation claims, and discrimination complaints. Most state and federal agencies count every day, including weekends and holidays, as part of the time limits.

Even people with the very best reasons for not filing their complaints on time are still required to follow the time limits. These limits are usually generous—180 days to file a discrimination complaint, and fifteen, thirty, sixty, or ninety days to appeal a ruling. The law rarely forces someone to react in a one- or two-day time period.

The problem is that some people procrastinate and put the paperwork aside, waiting for some divine intervention or for someone else to take the responsibility for filing the paperwork. There is absolutely nothing that can be done once that time limit is passed. Your case will not be heard.

Two years ago the company I worked for fired me without any notice because of my race. I didn't do anything right away because I have been sick. Can an attorney help me with my case now?

Sorry, no. Most state and federal agencies require that discrimination complaints be filed 180 to 300 days from the date of the violation. Those days include both weekends and holidays.

About eighteen months ago I was wrongfully terminated from my union job because of my race. I filed a grievance with the union, but they have been putting off a scheduled mediation with the company. Can an attorney help me?

Unfortunately, an attorney will not be able to help you. You must file a discrimination complaint with the EEOC 180 to 300 days after the date of the violation. The time does not stop being counted just because your union has offered to mediate the problem. Your union may be able to get you into mediation, but if the mediation is not successful, you will not be able to threaten that you will then file a complaint with the EEOC.

Unfortunately, this situation is rather common, especially in shops where the union has a close relationship with the company. By stalling the mediation until past the time when the employee is allowed to file a discrimination complaint, the company has little incentive to resolve the discrimination issue.

If a union employee feels that he or she has a valid discrimination complaint, he or she should have an attorney file the complaint within the required time period. Then if the mediation fails, the union employee will still be able to continue his or her EEOC complaint against the company.

Section II:
The Employee-Employer Relationship

Section II concentrates on the interactions between the employee and the employer. It begins in Chapter 5 with the hiring process, a point where an unknowledgeable employer can take many illegal actions. Once an employee is hired, there are actions by the employer, discussed in Chapter 6, which can be against the law. Finally we will discuss a new area of employment law—bullying—in Chapter 7.

Chapter 5

THE HIRING PROCESS

- Am I required to put all of my past employers on a job application?
- What can happen if I purposely do not include something or misstate something on a job application or on a resume, and am hired?
- Does every employer run professional background checks before hiring someone?
- What does a background check show?
- What type of information in a background check might be considered negative and prevent me from being hired?
- Is it legal for an employer to require drug testing, employment testing, or a certain level of education for a job? Doesn't that hurt certain races more than others?
- What can I do if my past employer is lying about me to potential employers?
- I was convicted of a minor crime. Will that hurt my chances of being hired?
- If my conviction keeps me from being hired, isn't that discrimination?
- Is it okay to just leave my criminal record off of my job application?
- I feel that I was not hired due to my race. What can I do about that?

Am I required to put all of my past employers on a job application?

You should not lie or omit information from a job application. In today's electronic world, a full background check is quick and easy for any employer to get. If a past employer paid you any salary, it will show up in a standard background check. Usually, employers consider those who leave something off an application to be less than honest, which can hurt a person in the hiring process and even after being hired.

What can happen if I purposely do not include something or misstate something on a job application or on a resume, and am hired?

Even after a person is hired, omissions or half-truths can still hurt. It is not unusual for an employer that is trying to cut expenses to look at the long-term employee who is making a significant salary. This may include revisiting the information the employee provided when he or she was hired. If the employee deliberately left some important factor out or included erroneous information on the application, the employer can terminate that employee without severance pay, even in the instance of a union or employment contract.

If there is a past job or a past legal incident that the employee feels will not look good to the employer, the best way to handle this is to be honest by providing the information up front and be prepared to provide a reasonable explanation. For example, a past job where the employee was fired must be listed. In the interview the employee can provide a neutral reason for the termination, such as, "The company was bought out and the new management wanted to get rid of the employees loyal to the previous employer." Remember that honesty is one of the qualities that employers value the most.

Does every employer run professional background checks before hiring someone?

While not every employer runs professional background checks before hiring someone, since they are getting easier to conduct and are getting less expensive, it is probable that more employers are using them. At a bare minimum, your potential employer will probably look you up on the Internet. It is pretty much standard operating procedure for an employer to Google any potential employees and to view anything that they have created about themselves, which includes entries made on Facebook and MySpace.

What does a background check show?

What is contained in a background check depends on the type of background check the employer has ordered. Minimally, it will list any jobs you have held, names you have used, and any criminal activity. Most employers also opt for a credit check to be included in the report as well.

What type of information in a background check might be considered negative and prevent me from being hired?

Many employers find any type of criminal conviction (misdemeanor or felony) to be a major negative mark against hiring a person. For some jobs—such as those dealing with securities, money, banking, or other public funds—there may be a federal or state legal requirement that an employee may not have a criminal record. For jobs without a specific legal requirement, an employer may have determined that a clean criminal record is a requirement for that particular job. It is legal for an employer to determine its own requirements for jobs as long as those requirements are enforced equally for all potential employees regardless of age, race, sex, nationality, religion, and disability.

Another issue that employers consider negative is having a poor credit report. Many employers feel that a person with poor credit may be tempted to steal from the employer. Again, this is a perfectly legal reason for not hiring someone as long as the employer equally enforces this requirement regardless of the potential employee's age, race, sex, nationality, religion, disability, or any discrimination basis that has been defined by the EEOC and the state law.

Is it legal for an employer to require drug testing, employment testing, or a certain level of education for a job? Doesn't that hurt certain races more than others?

Usually, Title VII—which is enforced by the EEOC—and the courts allow drug testing, employment testing, or the requirement of a certain level of education, unless these tests or requirements are done specifically to discriminate against one race.

Employment testing is legal as long as the employer does not administer what are called *race-norming employment tests*, which use different cutoff scores for different races. The test must be the same for every potential employee who is applying for this job, and all potential employees must be tested.

Educational requirements are also considered legal for a job requirement. The courts look at whether the requirement is a qualification for all applicants and whether these types of requirements exceed what is actually needed to perform the job.

What can I do if my past employer is lying about me to potential employers?

The answer to this question depends on state law. Some states will allow a past employer to say anything as long as the employer honestly believes that what it is saying is true. The majority of states limit the information allowed to be given out about a previous employee to the date hired, date separated, title or job position, and a few allow a salary range.

If you are in a state that allows the employer to say anything he or she wants or are concerned about what your supervisor will say, there are a few things you can do. If your previous employer has a human resources department, provide the potential employer with the phone number of that department. Those in the HR department are experienced in providing neutral information. If you are asked for the name of your supervisor, provide the name, but not that person's direct phone number, which will cut down on potential problems from a supervisor who holds a grudge.

If there is no way around the potential employer speaking with your former supervisor—as in the case of a small company where there is no human resources department or where your supervisor is the owner—or if you know for sure that a former supervisor is saying negative things about you, you should prepare your potential employer. While you should be honest, you want to present this in the best possible light. For example, saying, "My supervisor and I had a personality conflict," is much better than going on about how mean and nasty your previous supervisor was to you. Along with that honesty, be prepared to provide this potential employer with the names and phone numbers of people who can provide good work references for you, such as other former supervisors.

Before you take a former employer to court, which can be very expensive, make sure that the former employer is really providing a poor reference. It could be that the potential employer has received erroneous information from one of your former co-workers, who is spreading rumors. Also, the potential employer could have misunderstood something said in a reference.

In most states, in order to successfully bring a lawsuit against a former employer, you will need testimony from a potential employer that has decided not to hire you based on what the former employer has said. The majority of potential employers will not be willing to get involved in any lawsuit, no matter how valid.

If you believe that your past employer is lying about you and keeping you from being offered new employment, you will have quite a lot to prove in court. This is where a local employment attorney can assist you in structuring your case in accordance with your state laws.

I was convicted of a minor crime. Will that hurt my chances of being hired?

In today's economy, the unfortunate answer is that being convicted of a crime will probably hurt your chances of being hired.

If you had a conviction when you were a minor, you may be able to get your record expunged of the conviction. The same thing may also be true in some other types of cases if the conviction was long ago, if the punishment was community service, or if the crime is considered minor. The best way to find out if you can get your record expunged is to have an attorney do the work for you.

If you cannot get your record expunged, be prepared to explain the conviction and your rehabilitation. Go into the interview with answers to questions about the conviction, show remorse, show that you have not gotten into trouble since that event, and show that you are now an upstanding member of the community.

If my conviction keeps me from being hired, isn't that discrimination?

Very few states include a criminal conviction as a discrimination basis for jobs where the employer would have no real reason not to hire someone who has a conviction on his or her record. However, today's society is extremely security-conscious and many employers will be able to provide legitimate business reasons for their decisions.

Is it okay to just leave my criminal record off of my job application?

Leaving your criminal record off your job application would be the worst thing that you could do. If you know that this conviction is still on your record, you need to let your potential employer know about it before it is discovered in a background check. If you do not let your potential employer know, he or she may believe that you attempted to lie or fraudulently hide this, which can hurt you.

I feel that I was not hired due to my race. What can I do about that?

One of the major reasons for the laws against discrimination is to prevent discrimination in hiring. Discrimination bases are determined by the EEOC and your state's human rights agency. Go to Chapter 8 in this book on discrimination and Chapter 10 on filing a discrimination complaint for more detailed information.

Chapter 6

ACTIONS THAT CAN AFFECT THE EMPLOYER-EMPLOYEE RELATIONSHIP

- Can my employer restructure my job without my consent?
- Can my hours be changed? Can I be penalized for needing to work a different schedule than my supervisor wants me to work?
- Can my employer require that I relocate to another division of the company or move to a different part of the country?
- My title was recently changed from Junior Vice President to Manager. My salary, duties, and office have not changed. Is it an act of discrimination for an employer to change a job title?
- Can my health care benefits be dropped?
- Can my employer fire me in order to hire a relative? Can my employer put a spouse or relative—who knows nothing about the company—in a management position?
- Does every employer need an employee handbook in order to hold the employees to a certain standard of rules?
- In a downsizing or layoff, can my employer let the long-term employees go before those who were just recently hired?
- I was accused of stealing, making sexual remarks, and violating a serious workplace rule, and was fired without being able to defend myself in an internal investigation. Did my employer violate my due process rights?
- Can my employer fire me because I was sick in the hospital, took off time due to an injury received on the job, or took off time due to pregnancy?
- Can my employer require a doctor's note every time I take a sick day and force me into incurring additional medical expenses?
- My employer wants me to call in sick every day, even when I already have a note from my doctor saying that I should be off for ten work days. Is this legal?

- Can my employer fire me because I made a mistake, purposely exaggerated my qualifications, or purposely left out a previous job where I was fired on my job application?
- Can my employer fire me because I used the computer at work to get some of my personal emails or accessed a website for my own personal use?
- Can my employer short my pay without reason? Can my employer pay females less than males for doing the same jobs?

Can my employer restructure my job without my consent?

If you are an at will employee, your employer can change the duties of your job. The employer can add more responsibilities, which often happens following downsizing, when every employee must take on the duties of those who were let go. Usually these additional duties do not come with a pay increase. If you are a salaried employee, a pay increase is not legally required. However, if you are paid on an hourly basis, and these additional duties require more than the normal eight-hour day, you may be eligible for overtime pay.

If your employer suddenly assigns additional tasks to your or reassigns you to different tasks, it may not be a negative. Most employers are eager to promote employees but are wary that the employee may not be able to take on additional responsibilities. Your boss may be giving you the extra work as a test to see if you can handle a promotion. It could also be that because of job cuts, your boss needs someone to step up and help get the work done that used be done by those who have left the company.

Either way, the best action is for the employee to take on the extra tasks and do his or her best with these new assignments. Do not assume that you are being punished because you have been given more work. It could be that you are being considered for a different job or that the boss trusts you to help out when the company needs more work done. Once you have mastered these extra tasks, you will be in a better position to discuss a reward—such as a raise—at your annual performance review.

An employer cannot legally restructure jobs as a way to get rid of a certain protected class of people. For example, an employer cannot add the task of lifting one hundred pounds to a job where no lifting has been required in order to get rid of females. Sometimes when there is a restructuring and a particular class of employees is disproportionately affected by those actions, it will take an EEOC complaint and trial to determine if the real reason for the restructuring was actually discrimination.

Can my hours be changed? Can I be penalized for needing to work a different schedule than my supervisor wants me to work?

Unfortunately, not only at will employees but sometimes union employees get caught in a situation where a shift is eliminated or the company switches to different hours. Many times even union contracts do not address how to protect the employees on the eliminated shift. A union or contract employee may be able to rely on a seniority clause in his or her contract, but at will employees are not protected.

The reality is that many times employees affected by a shift being eliminated or hours being changed are young mothers who must arrange their work hours in order to obtain child care. There is no law in the United States that gives additional rights to parents so they can reschedule hours around day care or child care. This type of change can also affect those who work two jobs and those who attend school.

Just as in the changing of job responsibilities, changing of hours or shift elimination cannot be done for discriminatory reasons. Also, like other legal disputes, this action may only be settled in court. Be warned however, the employer will swear and produce evidence that this type of change was done solely due to economic and business reasons. The EEOC does recognize economic and business reasons as legitimate arguments against discrimination.

Can my employer require that I relocate to another division of the company or move to a different part of the country?

Yes. Both at will employees and those under employment or union contracts may lose their jobs due to an employer moving out of state or closing. While some union contracts do require that the employer offer the employees at the closing workplace an equal job at another site, for most people moving is impossible.

If the employee can show discrimination on the part of the employer, though, the employee may be able to file a complaint with the EEOC and the state's human rights agency. If the work site is closing, if an entire department is being moved, or when many people are being relocated due to a business decision, though, this is very difficult to prove.

My title was recently changed from Junior Vice President to Manager. My salary, duties, and office have not changed. Is it an act of discrimination for an employer to change a job title?

In order for the courts to consider a title change as discriminatory, you would need to show that you were singled out for the title change because of a discrimination basis and the change caused a reduction in your salary or benefits.

The latest case on this came in April 2008, when the U.S. Court of Appeals for the Seventh Circuit found that a less prestigious title change was not considered an "adverse employment action" as long as salary and benefits remained the same. It is not uncommon for companies to rewrite all titles, especially when they have been bought by another corporation that has its own different set of titles. While it can be argued that a title gives an employee a level of prestige, courts have so far not placed a dollar amount on that prestige.

Can my health care benefits be dropped?

One of the really sad things about health care is that so far there are only some state laws and no federal laws that require employers to offer health care benefits for employees. As a nation, we are all hopeful that a future administration will resolve the health care benefits issue so that it becomes fair for everyone—employer and employee.

One of the most prevalent problems in health care benefits is the huge increase in premiums that employers and employees must pay to receive even the most minimal of insurance coverage. These prices undergo annual increases that eliminate any raise or cost of living increase the employee may have gotten. With no end of these increases in sight, some employers are eliminating this benefit altogether or trying to find other lower-cost alternatives. One of the most recent methods that employers are taking to lower insurance costs is to penalize those employees who do things that may or may not affect their health, specifically smoking or being overweight. The federal law under Title I and Title V of the Americans with Disabilities Act of 1990 does not allow discrimination based a person's disability. Additionally, other federal and state laws have carved out *bases of discrimination*—things that an employer cannot base terminations or disciplinary actions on. None of these laws protect the rights of smokers or people who are overweight, so they have become the latest targets.

Can my employer fire me in order to hire a relative? Can my employer put a spouse or relative—who knows nothing about the company—in a management position?

Unless a union contract or employment contract specifically prohibits this act—called nepotism—the employer is within his or her legal rights to hire a relative or promote a relative within the company. This practice causes many complaints by employees who feel that they are being unfairly singled out. While it may be unfair, neither the federal government nor state governments consider this act to be discriminatory on its face.

That being said, if the employee can point to a particular discrimination basis, there may be sufficient evidence to file a complaint with the EEOC and the state's human rights agency.

Does every employer need an employee handbook in order to hold the employees to a certain standard of rules?

Employers must have a method to communicate the policies and rules to their employees. However, this method is not limited by law. Having policies posted on bulletin boards, listed on the company's Intranet, issued in memos to all employees, and published in the handbook have all be deemed as legal methods of communication. Any method that allows all employees to freely access the rules and policies of the employer will probably be accepted by the court. The primary issue with rules and policies is that they are applied equally to every employee.

In a downsizing or layoff, can my employer let the long-term employees go before those who were just recently hired?

Seniority is meaningless unless the employee has a union or employment contract that specifically makes seniority an important issue. There is no legal protection for an employee who devotes all of his or her working life to one employer. Even unions are starting to back off from making seniority an important factor in their contracts.

In a downsizing or layoff where money is the biggest issue, the longer an employee has been with a company—and the larger his or her salary—the more likely it is that employee will be let go, because if the employer is being pressured to reduce expenses, it is easier to terminate a few highly-paid employees than it is to actually try and make other cost-cutting moves. Once the highly-paid employee is gone, his or her salary amount is no longer considered an expense.

I was accused of stealing, making sexual remarks, and violating a serious workplace rule, and was fired without being able to defend myself in an internal investigation. Did my employer violate my due process rights?

For all those *Law & Order* viewers, the due process rights apply only in criminal cases and in very rare federal government employment cases. An employer is not legally required to prove anything in order to terminate an at will employee. While the EEOC does encourage employers to conduct some sort of a reasonable investigation, it is not mandatory. Since any investigation conducted by an employer is not done under the supervision of the courts, the accused employee does not have the legal right to be heard or to present a case.

Can my employer fire me because I was sick in the hospital, took off time due to an injury received on the job, or took off time due to pregnancy?

These are complex issues that do not always turn out to be fair for the employee. Generally, an employer has a legal right to demand that the employee show up for work. In the courts, the issue of absenteeism is usually decided in favor of the employer. The employer can legally limit the number of sick days allowed to each employee and can legitimately terminate an employee who goes over that number. When that employee applies for unemployment benefits, all states allow the employer to fight against awarding those benefits because of excessive absenteeism.

Excessive absenteeism does not depend on how legitimate the employee's illness is. It is legal for the employer to require a doctor's note for any absences due to illness; however, that note does not absolve the employee from taking the time off. Courts side with the employer when it comes to issues of sick time.

As for an injury that occurred on the job, if the employee has filed a workers' compensation claim, there is some protection under state laws during the time that the employee cannot work. Employers can legally require that an employee under the protection of a workers' compensation claim go to the employer's doctors for evaluations. Some employees feel that these doctors will not be accurate in their evaluations, and many times the employer's and employee's doctors differ in diagnosis and the date for the employee to return to work. Problems can also arise when the employee attempts to return to his or her job if it either has been eliminated or the employee is no long physically able to perform it.

Regarding those who are terminated due to taking time off for a pregnancy, this can fall under the umbrella of excessive absenteeism, especially when the employer does not offer pregnancy leave. The

EEOC prohibits discrimination due to pregnancy, as do most states. The employee will need to prove that she was not provided with the same time off as other employees received who had a temporary illness. She must show that the termination was due to her pregnancy and not to the issue of excessive absenteeism.

Pregnancy discrimination, disability discrimination, and discrimination against those who have filed workers' compensation claims are complex matters that must be individually evaluated by a local attorney.

Can my employer require a doctor's note every time I take a sick day and force me into incurring additional medical expenses?

As long as you are an at will employee, your employer can force you to get a doctor's note for each and every day you are sick. This is one of the latest corporate ideas to curb employees' taking days off.

My employer wants me to call in sick every day, even when I already have a note from my doctor saying that I should be off for ten work days. Is this legal?

Yes it is. Most employers have rules that employees must call in sick every day they aren't coming into work, and if they do not, the employees can be terminated. Even in cases where the employee has a doctor's note that says that he or she must not work for a period of time, it is up to the employer to decide whether the employee still must make that call. If this is the rule in your company, and you are in the situation where you will be off sick for a period of time you should:

1. make sure that your boss, manager, and human resources department each have a copy of the doctor's note; and,

2. ask if you are required to make that daily call.

Can my employer fire me because I made a mistake, purposely exaggerated my qualifications, or purposely left out a previous job where I was fired on my job application?

Any error, no matter how small or innocent, can legally be considered as grounds for termination due to dishonesty. This can be made even worse when the error is a deliberate attempt to add degrees or education.

The bigger problem comes when the employee has been working at the company for many, many years after this mistake was made, only to have truth come out. This often happens when one company is bought out by another one. It is common for the new company to review the employment file of each employee whom they obtained through the merger. Applications are verified, resumes are looked at, degrees are questioned. Many times the new company will find something that is wrong in the original resume or application. They will use this past dishonesty as a reason to terminate the employee.

Can my employer fire me because I used the computer at work to get some of my personal emails or accessed a website for my own personal use?

Not only can the employer terminate you, but if there is a company rule against using the computer for nonbusiness reasons, you may have problems getting unemployment benefits. The reason for this is that the computer, its software, and the access to the Internet are all considered to be company property. Many employers consider using their computers for an employee's own purpose a form of stealing. Additionally, you are being paid to work and do the assignments for the employer.

Many employers are now monitoring the websites that their employees access during work hours to make sure they are doing work. This is not against the law; in fact, the courts have specifically allowed employers to do this.

Can my employer short my pay without reason? Can my employer pay females less than males for doing the same jobs?

The issue of pay and being paid a fair wage is very important. The EEOC enforces the Equal Pay Act of 1963 (EPA), which protects men and women who perform substantially equal work in the same establishment from sex-based wage discrimination. Many states have similar laws. In addition, the Department of Labor enforces the laws that make it illegal to not pay employees the compensation that they are legally due. It provides at least three forums for the employee to report employers that short pay, do not pay commission, do not pay fairly, or who do not make good on bounced paychecks.

Many times the issue of a commission, bonus, or raise that is not paid occurs after a person is no longer employed with that company. It is standard operating procedures for employers to set up rules on the payment of commissions, bonuses, and even raises, that require an employee to remain employed for a particular length of time. An example of how this can happen is that the employee earns a commission, bonus, or raise that is not paid out until the end of the year. Before the final workday of that year the employee quits and expects that the commission, bonus, or raise will be sent to him or her after the year-end accounting is performed. The employer has set up rules that this commission, bonus, or raise will only be distributed if the employee works thirty, sixty, or ninety days into the new year. For the most part, courts have found that this type of arrangement is legal as long as it is administered to all employees equally. Your state laws and your circumstances may differ. Only a local employment attorney can review your case and the current law.

Chapter 7

BULLYING IN THE WORKPLACE

- What is workplace bullying?
- Is workplace bullying against the law?
- What exactly is bullying? If my boss yells, "You're late!" am I being bullied?
- Why don't employers fire bullies?
- Is it a violation of discrimination laws for a supervisor to create a hostile work environment?
- What can an employee do when his or her supervisor is a bully?
- What should an employee do if the bully slaps or hits him or her?
- What happens if I quit because my supervisor bullied me to a point where I could not take going into work another day?
- When will bullying at work be against the law?

What is workplace bullying?

Workplace bullying is the creation of a hostile work environment by someone—management or co-workers—who yells, screams, intimidates, berates, insults, humiliates, threatens, or initiates any verbal or physical conduct that a reasonable person would find as disturbing, threatening, or hostile. The most common type of bullying is verbal, but there are not current laws against verbal bullying. However, if the bullying becomes physical, then the criminal laws—such as the laws prohibiting assault and battery—can be used to stop the bullying.

Is workplace bullying against the law?

Currently, acts of bullying are only against the law if the bully bases his or her actions on discrimination, which are limited to age, sex, race, color, nationality, disability, or religion. If a bully were to pick on a person due to discrimination, then it would be easy to rid the workplace of its bullies. However, because this is usually not the case, it is very hard to get rid of a workplace bully.

What exactly is bullying? If my boss yells, "You're late!" am I being bullied?

Bullying is more than an occasional loud comment in a situation where the employee has made a mistake. It is a continuous lack of respect of the employee by someone who is abusive. One of the reasons that we do not currently have laws against bullying is because it is so hard to define. What is abusive or bullying to one person may be just considered a minor annoyance to another.

Bullies tend to overreact to any error or perceived error of others. Bullies carry a grudge or annoyance due to something done by others—or something the bully perceived was done by others, for much longer and at a much higher intensity than what normal people do. Bullies will use demeaning or curse words when talking to their victims. Bullies think nothing of embarrassing their victims in front of others, even to the point where it makes the bullies look bad. A bully will not allow the victim to state his or her side of an issue; it is the bully's way or nothing. Bullies tend to take credit for everything that is right and place blame on others for wrongs that the bullies have created. Bullies have little or no empathy for anyone and can single-handedly destroy the morale of a hard-working employee, department, or even an entire company.

Why don't employers fire bullies?

Many employers are hesitant to get rid of bullies for a number of reasons. It is not unusual for a bully to be the owner or the top executive of a company. He or she is given a certain respect and allowed to go on tirades because the bully reports to no one.

In some companies, the bully is the nag, enforcer, or pusher who does the dirty work for the bosses. This type of bully has been given an unspoken authority by bosses who prefer to be liked by all employees. It is easier for managers to allow the bully to do the job of keeping the workers productive than for them to get involved with day-to-day motivation and work problems.

Bullies can also be hardworking, long-term employees who feel they have earned their positions as chief enforcers. Because of his or her experience with a company, the bully may know more about how to do things than the supervisor does. The bully may also be the only person in a small company who knows how to do certain tasks. This makes it easier for management to just turn its head and ignore the bullying, especially since bullying is not against the law and the work is getting done.

The problem is that many employers underestimate the major destruction that a bully causes. These employers that look the other way when it comes to bullying only see the minor benefits that the bully gives them in handling unpleasant tasks and keeping the organization working. However, the employer must understand that the problems are being covered up and productivity is probably not as high as it could be if employees were not perpetually feeling bullied. Allowing bullying to continue will also probably chase away the good workers who not only take pride in their work but value themselves. Eventually the company can get a negative reputation as a miserable place to work, which will cause a company to have to give a higher salary just to keep people. A bully can be a major financial drain in the long term for any employer.

Is it a violation of discrimination laws for a supervisor to create a hostile work environment?

Currently a hostile workplace is only used in terms of the current discrimination bases, the most common being sexual harassment (the demanding of sexual favors by an employer). As the law stands today, unless there is a link from the bullying to some recognized discrimination basis, the employee cannot claim discrimination or a hostile work environment.

Many times an employee suffers from a bullying boss to the point where the employee must be under the care of a doctor. A physical problem brought on by the bullying can sometimes be used as part of a discrimination complaint; however, this really depends on the circumstances of the case.

What can an employee do when his or her supervisor is a bully?

Until laws are enacted that specifically prohibit verbal bullying, an employee who is subjected to a bully may have few legal options. As with any workplace issue, the first thing is to report the problem to the human resources department. A real effort should be made to tie the bullying to one of the bases of discrimination. The employee who is being bullied must make the employer see that allowing the bullying to continue will affect the bottom line, either through litigation or the loss of productivity. Right now, though, that may be a losing battle. Because the issue of bullying in the workplace is changing, an employee who is subjected to bullying should contact a local employment attorney before making any drastic moves.

What should an employee do if the bully slaps or hits him or her?

Any time anyone in the workplace touches another person inappropriately, it is grounds for filing a police complaint. Some bullies go from excessive verbal abuse to physical attacks, shoving, or hitting. Once the bully touches the victimized employee, that employee must report it to the proper authorities. In some workplaces, the proper authorities may be a security force that is part of the company, while in others it will be the local police. Make no mistake—your employer will not be happy if you bring in the police, but it is against the law to be inappropriately touched by anyone. In addition, many state laws specifically require that employers keep their employees safe from physical attacks.

What happens if I quit because my supervisor bullied me to a point where I could not take going into work another day?

First, before you quit, make sure that you have filed a formal complaint with the human resources department or your supervisor's manager. A formal complaint lists all grievances in writing. Make note of the date that this document was provided to human resources and management. Do not assume that everyone knows about the bully. Even if they do, in order to legally protect yourself, you need to put your grievance in writing and formally present it to your employer.

Second, see if someone in human resources or the supervisor's manager will take your side and assist in stopping the bullying. You must give people adequate time to respond to your request for action. Follow up with these people. Ask what is being done to solve the problem and when you can expect to see a change in behavior. Be polite and patient, but be determined to end the bullying.

Third, if human resources or management refuses to stop the bullying or is unable to change it, then—again in writing—request a different job that will keep you away from the bully. If there is nowhere for you to go, then you need to do two more things:

1. have a local employment attorney review your case to see if the law allows charges to be brought; and,

2. start looking for another job.

In many employment cases, the employer will come to any legal hearing with the excuse of not knowing about the problem. It is up to the employee to prove with evidence—such as copies of written complaints given to human resources—that not only did the employer know about the bullying, but the employer did nothing to stop the problem.

A strong word of caution here. Those of us who have been victimized by the bully boss get to that point where all we really want to do is to run away from the problem. It takes courage to stand and fight even when you are in the right. While running away is a very good survival instinct, you really should try to work things out in the above manner before quitting your job. The majority of states do not allow a person to collect unemployment benefits if he or she quits, so unless you have a job lined up, try and stick it out.

When will bullying at work be against the law?

Bullying is the next hot topic in employment law. For many years the only protection that an employee had against a mean, unfair, or miserable supervisor was when that supervisor's actions fell under a basis of discrimination. That is slowly changing, but the change is not happening very quickly.

According to the Workplace Bullying Institute, about 54 million Americans have been victimized by workplace bullies. So far thirteen states have introduced legislation into their legislatures that will make workplace bullying illegal, but currently none of these states have enacted any laws to protect an employee from bullying.

<u>More information on bullying</u>

• Workplace Bullying Institute, **www.bullyfreeworkplace.org**

• Healthy Workplace Advocates:
  • In New York: **www.nyhwa.org**
  • In Vermont: **www.vtbullybusters.org**
  • In Maryland: **www.mdstopbully.com**

Section III:
Common Violations of
Employment Laws

This section looks in detail at the protection employees receive from the most often used employment laws. Chapter 8 is subdivided into the discrimination bases as determined by the EEOC. In this chapter, we look at each discrimination basis and provide information about what needs to proven to the EEOC, the evidence an employee needs to provide, and details about what the courts look at in each type of discrimination case. Chapter 9 briefly touches on other nondiscrimination violations of employment laws.

Chapter 8

DISCRIMINATION

- Are there any rules or requirements that apply to filing all types of discrimination complaints?
- Why are you concentrating on federal law? What about state laws?
- When you say "discriminatory practice," what actions are you talking about?

Age Discrimination

- What is age discrimination?
- What does an employee need to prove age discrimination?
- My new manager made a speech to all employees about how he was going to get rid of the old methods, old ideas, old goals, and the old guard. Do the employees who are over 40 years old have a case for age discrimination?

Racial Discrimination

- What is racial discrimination?
- What does racial discrimination include?
- What is color discrimination?
- Can an employee file a complaint because of being harassed about his or her race?
- What are examples of severe or pervasive conduct?
- Is it racial discrimination to be fired for associating with another race?
- Are there other workplace actions that can be used to prove racial discrimination in a complaint?

Disability Discrimination

- What is disability discrimination?
- What is needed to prove disability discrimination?
- What are major life activities?
- What are reasonable accommodations?
- What can an employer ask a disabled applicant?

- Does the ADA consider someone who is dependent on illegal drugs to be disabled?
- How does the association discrimination section of the Americans with Disabilities Act work?

Equal Pay Discrimination
- What is equal pay discrimination?
- Sounds like equal pay discrimination is just part of discrimination due to a person's sex. Is this true?

National Origin Discrimination
- What is national origin discrimination?
- Does that mean that employers that have an English-only rule are guilty of national origin discrimination?
- Isn't national origin discrimination the same as race discrimination?

Religious Discrimination
- What is religious discrimination?
- How can you determine reasonable accommodations?
- How can I prove that my employer did not provide religious accommodations?
- I asked for certain days off to follow my religion, and my boss asked for a written explanation of the celebration and information on my religion. Is this religious discrimination?
- My boss told me that I may not teach scripture to my co-workers during work hours, but this is part of what I must do in my religion. Am I being discriminated against?
- I am not allowed to wear a religious head-covering to work. Is this religious discrimination?
- Can an atheist file a religious discrimination complaint?

Retaliation
- What is retaliation? Is it the same as whistle-blowing violations?
- How do I prove retaliation?

Sex Discrimination

- What is sex discrimination? How does it differ from sexual harassment?
- How can I prove that I have been discriminated against due to my sex or that I have been the victim of sexual harassment?
- Does the fact that I willingly had sexual relations with my boss hurt my complaint of sexual harassment? I tried to stop the affair, but he continues to pressure me for sex.
- My male boss has made sexual advances toward me (also male), including grabbing my behind and talking about homosexual sex. Is this sexual harassment?

Pregnancy Discrimination

- What is pregnancy discrimination?
- What law covers pregnancy discrimination?
- My job has pregnancy and birth benefits, but it is limited to those who are married. Is this pregnancy discrimination?
- My boss will not give me time off—even unpaid—for my problem pregnancy and for the time after the baby is born. Is this pregnancy discrimination?
- Can my employer change my job and pay me less because I am pregnant?
- My employer has cut my hours and pay since I revealed that I was pregnant. Is this legal?

Family Responsibility and Caregiver Discrimination

- What is family responsibility or caregiver discrimination?
- What does this new interpretation of the existing laws do?
- Does that make the caregiver or parent a new protected class with the EEOC?
- Where can I get more information on caregiver discrimination?

Are there any rules or requirements that apply to filing all types of discrimination complaints?

There are three primary rules that can easily trip a person up in filing a discrimination complaint and prevent the EEOC from even accepting a complaint.

1. The first rule deals with the length of time from the incident you are complaining about to the day you file the complaint. Currently, the EEOC will allow a person to file a complaint up to three hundred days after an incident (such as termination). The three-hundred-day time limit includes weekends and holidays. It may be helpful for you to use a calendar when determining if your complaint fits within this time limit. There are no exceptions for complaints that are filed too late.

2. The second rule is the requirement that an employer must employ a minimum of twenty or more people for complaints of age discrimination to be heard. All other discrimination charges require that an employer employ a minimum of fifteen people. An employee may need to determine how many workers the employer had at the time of the alleged discrimination, in order to comply with this requirement.

3. The third requirement is that a discrimination complaint must concern at least one of the bases that EEOC has set out as illegal discrimination. These bases are age, color, race, national origin, disability, religion, retaliation, or sex discrimination. No matter how egregious or unfair the actions of an employer are, they must be linked to one of these bases.

Why are you concentrating on federal law? What about state laws?

Federal laws apply to all states, and the vast majority of states also include all of the EEOC bases of discrimination in their state laws on discrimination. In the state's own discrimination laws, it is able to include additional bases of discrimination. For example, many states are now including military discrimination and sexual orientation discrimination as additional discrimination bases in their laws.

States cannot take away any of the discrimination bases listed in the federal laws—these bases must be followed in every state. States are allowed to:

1. set up their own discrimination laws that mirror the federal laws;

2. set up their own discrimination laws that not only mirror the federal laws but add some additional bases; or,

3. merely reference the federal law and run all discrimination complaints through the local federal agency office.

The appendices in the back of this book have more specific information on each state.

When you say "discriminatory practice," what actions are you talking about?

The actions that can be considered to be based on discrimination are:

- hiring;

- pay;

- benefits;

- task assignments;

- sick days and disability allocations;

- job classifications;

- training programs;

- promotions;

- overtime assignments;

- shift assignments;

- transfers;

- use of company facilities;

- layoffs;

- terminations;

- treatment by employer;

- retaliation;

- harassment;

- using stereotypes to make employee decisions;

- using a person's association with or marriage to a person of a particular race, religion, national origin, or disability to make employee decisions; and,

- any other terms or conditions of employment.

AGE DISCRIMINATION

What is age discrimination?

Age discrimination is when a person's age is used in an employment decision, unless age has been proven to be a bona fide job qualification. An example of a bona fide job qualification would be airline pilots who are limited by the FAA to a particular age.

The *Age Discrimination in Employment Act* (ADEA) specifically prohibits:

- age requirements on hiring notices;

- denying a person entry to apprenticeship programs due to his or her age;

- denying benefits to older employees; and,

- any of the discriminatory practices listed in the previous answer based on an employee's age (when the employee is over 40 years old).

What does an employee need to prove age discrimination?

Age discrimination is the hardest complaint to prove and the most prevalent in EEOC filings. It is hard to prove because the EEOC allows certain actions by the employer due to a sound business reason. It is true that when an employer is attempting to cut costs the easiest way to do that is to terminate the employees who make the most money. The employees who make the most money are most often those who are over 40 years old since they are often employed at a higher salary level. Courts would consider whether or not the termination was due to a business decision or due to the fact that the employee was over the age of 40 when determining whether age discrimination occurred.

Generally, to show discrimination, a person would need to show that other employees who were in the same or similar situation (such as same job duties or same title) and who were under 40 years old were not terminated or did not suffer the same action. Courts like to see something tangible that is also an indicator of an age bias, such as memos about age or a history of the employer terminating older workers in the past. However, age discrimination cases have been won without any additional paper evidence and with only the testimony of the employee who was discriminated against.

My new manager made a speech to all employees about how he was going to get rid of the old methods, old ideas, old goals, and the old guard. Do the employees who are over 40 years old have a case for age discrimination?

Probably not. The courts look at not just the word "old" but if it was directed at a particular person or if that person's name was used. Without any additional actions or speech directed at a specific person who is over 40 years old, it is doubtful that this would be considered age discrimination. However, in order to be sure, you may want to contact a local employment attorney to review the situation.

RACIAL DISCRIMINATION

What is racial discrimination?

Title VII, the law that prohibits the employer from acts that discrim-inate against persons because of race, does not define race. Courts have used race, ethnicity, and even national origin interchangeably.

What does racial discrimination include?

According to Title VII racial discrimination can generally include:

- ancestry—discrimination against an employee due to the race or national origin of his or her forefathers, even if the employee does not identify him- or herself as part of that race now;

- association—discrimination against an employee because he or she is friends with, dates, or is married to someone of a particular race;

- culture— discrimination against an employee because of his or her cultural characteristics, such as name, dress, appearance, or manner of speech;

- perception—discrimination against an employee because that employee is perceived to be part of a particular race, even though the employee does not identify him- or herself as part of that race;

- physical characteristics—discrimination against an employee due to certain physical attributes that are associated with a particular race;

- race-linked illnesses—discrimination against an employee who has a disease that is generally association with a particular race. For example, sickle cell anemia is commonly associated with those people of African descent. All employee illnesses must be treated equally;

- reverse racial discrimination—no race should be discriminated against. For years, many people associated Title VII only with protections for African Americans, which is wrong. All races are protected from discrimination under this law; and,

- subgroup discrimination—discrimination against an employee who is part of a subgroup within a particular race. Examples would be those who came from a certain town or village, those who are unmarried parents, etc. This overlaps with color discrimination and can overlap with all other discrimination bases listed above.

What is color discrimination?

While Title VII does not define color, courts have used this in situations where an employee has been discriminated against by a member of his or her own race because he or she has a too light or too dark skin tone. Again, race, color, and national origin can overlap, and each one should be considered when filing a discrimination complaint.

Can an employee file a complaint because of being harassed about his or her race?

Yes. Failure to provide a work environment free of racial harassment is discrimination under the law. In order to prove a racially hostile environment, the employee must show two things: unwelcome conduct and severe or pervasive conduct.

1. **Unwelcome conduct.** *Unwelcome conduct* is actions that the employee did not solicit, did not incite, and did not join in. For example, if an employee engaged in calling a co-worker by a racial slur and that co-worker retaliates by using a racial slur back, that is probably not unwelcome conduct. The court vigorously looks at the evidence and circumstances surrounding the conduct to determine if it was unwelcome.

2. **Severe or pervasive conduct.** In order to be a violation of Title VII, according to the Supreme Court, the racially abusive conduct must be more serious than being uncivil, but does not need to be something that causes monetary or psychological injury. This middle-of-the-road analysis means that every case is looked at individually. Some things that courts look at is the number of times this conduct occurred, whether there were physical threats, whether the purpose of the conduct was humiliation, whether the conduct interfered with the employee's work, and any other factor surrounding the conduct. Again, this something that the employee should seek the advice of an attorney to determine.

What are examples of severe or pervasive conduct?

Courts usually do not consider a single incident of racially offensive conduct or racially demeaning remarks as creating a hostile workplace. However, even a single incident can be considered severe if it involves physical harassment. Some examples of single incidents that courts have considered severe are:

- display of a noose;

- burning a cross;

- a favorable reference to the Ku Klux Klan;

- racial epithets; and,

- racial comparisons to an animal.

Is it racial discrimination to be fired for associating with another race?

Racial discrimination can extend to when an employee associates with, is dating, or is married to someone of another race. However, this is tough to prove. You will need concrete evidence to show that the employer singled you out due to you being in an interracial relationship. This is not a common case and should probably be handled by an experienced employment attorney.

Are there other workplace actions that can be used to prove racial discrimination in a complaint?

Workplace actions that can be used to prove racial discrimination begin at the hiring stage. Does the employer recruit and hire people without consideration of the potential employee's race? Once an employee is hired, are work assignments, perks, mentoring, and training provided to all employees regardless of race?

In regard to money, are the pay and options for pay increases structured so that every employee has the same opportunity to succeed? The courts have found racial discrimination in companies where a particular race is hired for only one or two types of jobs and those jobs have a lower pay base and raise percentage than all other jobs in the company.

In practice, are all employees given performance evaluations at the same interval? Are disciplinary actions or performance improvement plans given disproportionately to one race over another?

DISABILITY DISCRIMINATION

What is disability discrimination?

The Americans with Disabilities Act (ADA) is the law that prohibits discrimination due to a person's disability. It also enforces the concept of the employer providing a reasonable accommodation for someone with a disability.

What is needed to prove disability discrimination?

In order to prove disability discrimination, you first need to be an employee with a disability. The disability must be something that limits one or more major life activities. The individual must have a record of the disability and have informed the employer of this. In most cases, informing an employer is done by providing the employer with documentation from a health care professional.

Second, the disability must be something that is recognized as limiting major life activities—what in legal terms is called an *ADA-cognizable disability*. For example, a person with occasional headaches is not considered disabled because the occasional headache does not limit major life activities other than the few times a year when the headache comes on.

Third, the employee or potential employee must be a person who is qualified to do the job. This consideration is used when a disabled person applies for a job and is turned down due to his or her disability. The disabled person must possess the same qualifications for that job that the nondisabled person has. For example, if the job requires a license in a certain trade, not hiring a disabled person who does not possess that license is not a violation of the ADA.

Fourth, the employee must request a reasonable accommodation for his or her disability. This request usually comes from a doctor who indicates why this accommodation is necessary under standard medical practice.

Finally, the employer must refuse to grant the accommodation. However, the employer is allowed to refuse to grant an accommodation that puts an undue hardship on the employer's business. The determination of whether something is an *undue hardship* includes looking at the costs, size of the company, financial soundness of the business, and the nature and structure of the employer's location.

What are major life activities?

Major life activities are things that an average person can do with little or no problem. Specifically, courts have considered walking, breathing, seeing, hearing, speaking, learning, and working as major life activities.

What are reasonable accommodations?

Reasonable accommodations are determined by the court examining what is needed by this specific individual in order to do the job. This can be wheelchair accessibility, a particular supportive desk chair, lowering of work stations, restructuring the job, changing hours, providing or modifying equipment, or any other request made.

The reasonableness is determined by the employer. Issues like cost, the facility, and the size of a company are all considered. The courts will not impose an accommodation on an employer that causes an undue hardship. *Undue hardships* are defined as things that require significant difficulty or expense when measured according to the company's work and size. For example, it is unreasonable for a small accounting firm in a third-floor rented office in a walkup to install an elevator for a disabled employee. However, it may be reasonable to allow that person to do his or her work from home via computer equipment that is provided and paid for by the employer.

What can an employer ask a disabled applicant?

Generally, an employer can ask the same questions of a disabled applicant that he or she can ask a nondisabled applicant, specifically, "Can you do this job?" The employer cannot ask about the existence, nature, or severity of the disability. The employer can ask about the applicant's ability to perform the job function. The employer can make a conditioned job offer that is dependent on the results of a medical examination only when all applicants must pass the same medical examination.

Does the ADA consider someone who is dependent on illegal drugs to be disabled?

No. Employees and job applicants who currently use illegal drugs are not protected by the ADA. In addition, tests for illegal use of drugs are not considered medical examinations and are not subject to the ADA's restrictions of medical examinations. Employees who use illegal drugs or who have alcoholism are held to the same standards of performance as all other employees and cannot use the ADA to resolve the illegal drug or alcohol issue.

How does the association discrimination section of the Americans with Disabilities Act work?

This is a new section of the ADA that has already caused a lot of litigation. It is actually a very fair law for the employees. Originally, the ADA had three requirements for what was a protected disability, which was that the employee:

1. must have a physical or mental impairment that substantially limits one or more major life activities;

2. must have a record of such an impairment; and,

3. is regarded as having such an impairment or disability.

The new section of the ADA also includes employees who have a relationship or an association with an individual who has a disability. This new piece of the law protects an employee from being terminated because of his or her association with a disabled person. This usually applies when the disabled person is the spouse or child of the employee and the employee has the benefit of health insurance from his or her employer. The relationship with the disabled person causes the health care costs to rise for this employee and employers are anxious to cut rising expenses.

So far there has been only one serious case to test this law. The judge in that case also looked at the employer's repeated inquiries into the health of the dependent and suggestions that the employee look for another health care insurance. This is a to-be-watched issue that may finally bring some fairness to the employee who is not only a caregiver but provides the health care insurance through the employer.

EQUAL PAY DISCRIMINATION

What is equal pay discrimination?
This is covered by the Equal Pay Act of 1963. Equal pay discrimination is discrimination on the basis of sex in paying wages and providing benefits. The employees of both sexes must be performing work of similar skill, effort, and responsibility under the same or similar working conditions.

Sounds like equal pay discrimination is just part of discrimination due to a person's sex. Is this true?
A complaint of equal pay discrimination can be part of a sex discrimination complaint. In that case there are two claims—one about discrimination due to the person's sex and the second about

pay inequality. In most cases where the employee is complaining about inequality of pay, there are other incidents of discrimination that do not involve pay, such as women getting less training than men doing the same job, or women not being provided with the same tools or benefits as men. The creators of the Equal Pay Act of 1963 thought that the pay issue was so important that they created this law, which is found in Volume 29 of the United States Code at section 206(d).

NATIONAL ORIGIN DISCRIMINATION

What is national origin discrimination?

National origin discrimination is any discriminatory practice that is based on a person's birthplace, ancestry, culture, ancestral dress, or linguistic characteristics.

Does that mean that employers that have an English-only rule are guilty of national origin discrimination?

Employers with an English-only rule in the workplace may be guilty of national original discrimination, but it really depends on the individual case. If the employer can show that the English-only requirement is necessary for conducting business, then it may not be considered discrimination. The employer must inform applicants for a job that this rule exists, or if instituting the rule later, the employer must inform all workers of the rule and provide a certain amount of time for the workers to comply.

Isn't national origin discrimination the same as race discrimination?

National origin discrimination is not the same thing as race discrimination, but the two can be very close. In fact, one of the reasons to go to an employment attorney is so that the discrimination bases that overlap in your case can be identified and written up as separate causes of action. The EEOC has stated that discrimination by color, national origin, race, and religion can exist and overlap in one case. It is very important that you protect your rights in a discrimination complaint by identifying each potential discrimination basis that applies in your case.

RELIGIOUS DISCRIMINATION

What is religious discrimination?

Religious discrimination is considered a failure to accommodate a person's religion. By law the employer must make reasonable accommodations for an employee to practice his or her religion.

The issue that usually ends up in court is what is considered reasonable, and the answer to that question can vary depending on the facts of the case and the employer. Many times a religious discrimination case will go to mediation, where a compromise can be worked out between the employee and the employer.

How can you determine reasonable accommodations?

To determine reasonable accommodations, the courts look at the details of the employer, the size of the company, what the employee requested, how crucial this employee is to the business, how other employees of different religions are treated, and all other details surrounding this case. Courts probably will not force the employer to put the business in jeopardy to accommodate a key employee's extended absenteeism, but they may require that the employer be flexible in that person's working hours so that the employee can leave early for church services and make up the time on another day.

How can I prove that my employer did not provide religious accommodations?

To prove that your employer did not provide religious accommodations, you will need to show that you formally requested a certain religious accommodation and were refused. You may also want to list other employees who are doing the same or similar job as you and who are allowed religious accommodations.

I asked for certain days off to follow my religion, and my boss asked for a written explanation of the celebration and information on my religion. Is this religious discrimination?

No. It is not unusual for an employer to ask for some written information as to why you want certain time off, especially in the cases of religious celebrations that are not well known or religions that are new. Religious discrimination occurs when the employer refuses to allow a person to practice his or her religion, which can mean refusing to let the person work certain hours so he or she can be home by sundown or refusing to allow an employee to wear a head-covering.

My boss told me that I may not teach scripture to my co-workers during work hours, but this is part of what I must do in my religion. Am I being discriminated against?

You are probably not being discriminated against. Title VII's prohibition against discrimination based on religion applies to both you and your co-workers. Your co-workers have the same rights to their own religions and to not hear about your religion during work. Your employer must make a decision that will protect the rights of all the employees, even the co-workers who are of a different religion than you. What to you is being done out of kindness and a commitment to your faith, may be offensive to another person who has a different faith.

In addition, during work hours you are being paid to work and to follow the employer's orders. The employer is in its legal rights to expect that during working hours you will put your energy into your assigned tasks.

I am not allowed to wear a religious head-covering to work. Is this religious discrimination?

Unless your employer is not allowing a certain head-covering due to a safety issue, you are probably being subjected to religious discrimination. Additionally, you may also have a case for racial discrimination, if your religion is tied to a particular race or ethnic origin. You may want to have a local employment attorney look at your case to see if there are other issues, especially involving your state's laws.

Can an atheist file a religious discrimination complaint?

Right now, there is no definitive answer to this question. However, there are a few cases that are working their way through some state courts right now. Whether or not religious discrimination is found will probably be determined by the actions of the employer, and whether or not the employer was vigorously promoting a particular religion.

RETALIATION

What is retaliation? Is it the same as whistle-blowing violations?

Retaliation is an adverse action by an employer against an employee due to the employee reporting the employer for breaking the law.

There are three essential elements of a retaliation claim.

1. The employee participated in a protected activity, such as being witness to a co-worker's EEOC complaint, filing his or her own EEOC complaint, or reporting an illegal activity of the employer to the proper authorities.

2. The employer adversely treated the employee for the above action. This treatment must be a serious reaction by the employer, such as termination, demotion, discipline, or any event that negatively affects the employee's wages.

3. There is a connection between what the employee did and what the employer responded with. This usually involves closeness in time, or an actual admission by the employer.

Many states have whistle-blower laws that protect employees— including state employees—from retaliation for reporting a violation of law to the proper authorities. Those state laws are based on this same EEOC analysis.

How do I prove retaliation?

In order to prove retaliation, the first thing an employee must do is either participate in a legal complaint or report an employer's violation to the proper authority. Courts have found that merely reporting the employer internally within the company does not prove retaliation. The employee must have involved a government agency or be a participant in another worker's complaint to a government agency.

The employee must show that the action done by the employer against the employee was serious and was prompted by the reporting of the employer to the authorities. For example, a disciplinary action that was written up about an employee but was not put into effect until after the employee had filed an EEOC complaint would probably not be considered retaliation.

SEX DISCRIMINATION

What is sex discrimination? How does it differ from sexual harassment?

Sex discrimination in the workplace is when discriminatory practices are based on a person's gender. An example of this could be not providing female attorneys with desks, but providing male attorneys with desks and private offices, when each attorney has equal standing in the law firm.

Sexual harassment includes direct requests for sex and threatened actions if the employee does not comply. It can also include creating a hostile workplace through sexual banter, sexually-explicit photographs displayed in front of other employees, or other visual or auditory noises that are sexual in nature.

How can I prove that I have been discriminated against due to my sex or that I have been the victim of sexual harassment?

To prove sex discrimination, you will need to show that other employees who are of the opposite sex and who do the same or similar job as you are treated better. Better treatment can be that the other employees were not disciplined or terminated for doing the exact same action that caused you to be terminated or disciplined.

For sexual harassment, you need to show that you complained to your boss, your human resources department, or management about the sexual harassment. To protect your rights, this complaint or grievance should be in writing. Many times an employer will deny that any conversation about sexual harassment ever took place. Write down your complaints, and keep a copy with the date that you made the report. You should also give the employer a certain amount of time to stop the sexual harassment. Most courts prefer you to give your employer a few weeks to fix the problem.

Does the fact that I willingly had sexual relations with my boss hurt my complaint of sexual harassment? I tried to stop the affair, but he continues to pressure me for sex.

You need to be honest with your attorney and with the courts about your willing participation in sexual relations. This fact will come out, so you need to prepare your attorney for this. Your attorney will then be able to craft a theory or argument to protect you.

The reality is that this may hurt your case, but only if it could be perceived that filing this complaint was done as a way to get back at someone who no longer wanted to have a relationship with you.

You will need to testify that you wanted to stop the sexual relations but felt pressured for sex from a person who had the power over your livelihood. This is especially true if the boss threatened to fire you or give you a poor performance rating or do anything that would hurt your job unless you let him have his way.

My male boss has made sexual advances toward me (also male), including grabbing my behind and talking about homosexual sex. Is this sexual harassment?

Yes. The laws about sexual harassment include same-sex harassment. In addition, your state may have already passed a law that makes it illegal to discriminate due to a person's sexual orientation. Therefore, you may have multiple discrimination claims. A local employment attorney will be able to review your case along with all current state and federal discrimination laws.

PREGNANCY DISCRIMINATION

What is pregnancy discrimination?

Pregnancy discrimination is any discriminatory practice that is based on a person being pregnant, previous childbirth, and any related medical condition related to the pregnancy. The employer must treat a pregnant employee exactly the same as employees who have temporary illnesses or conditions. Generally, employers cannot refuse to hire a pregnant woman because of the pregnancy, cannot force a pregnant woman to go on medical leave until delivery of the baby, or in any manner treat a pregnant woman any differently than employees who have a temporary illness or disability.

What this means in the real world is that the employer is only required to hold open a pregnant woman's job if the employer also holds open jobs for those who are on medical leave. The employer cannot provide extra benefits for the pregnant worker beyond what is provided for all other workers.

What law covers pregnancy discrimination?

The Pregnancy Discrimination Act is an amendment to Title VII of the Civil Rights Act of 1964. Discrimination based on pregnancy is unlawful sex discrimination, because pregnancy only happens to females. Because pregnancy discrimination falls under the sex discrimination part of Title VII, an employer must employ a minimum of fifteen people in order to be subjected to this law. This law applies to state and local government employees, employees of employment agencies and labor organizations, and employees of the federal government.

My job has pregnancy and birth benefits, but it is limited to those who are married. Is this pregnancy discrimination?

This could be pregnancy discrimination, depending on the circumstances of your particular case. In general, any pregnancy-related benefits cannot be limited to those who are married. This includes health insurance that reimburses expenses.

> **Note:** There have been a few recent decisions about pregnancy discrimination where the courts have allowed an employer to terminate an employee who has never been married because of her pregnancy. In these cases, the employer was a faith-based company, the employee signed a contract that contained a morals clause that required following this faith's teachings about sex outside of marriage, and the pregnant employee had direct contact with children.

My boss will not give me time off—even unpaid—for my problem pregnancy and for the time after the baby is born. Is this pregnancy discrimination?

The law requires that employers treat pregnancy the exact same way they treat other short-term disabilities. The law does not require an employer to have a pregnancy leave policy. When determining if someone is being discriminated against due to pregnancy, the courts look at how the employer treats employees who have serious illnesses or injuries. So, if the employer does not offer unpaid time off to employees with illnesses or injuries, you probably do not have a pregnancy discrimination case.

You may be covered by the Family Medial Leave Act (FMLA), though, which can provide a limited amount of leave that is unpaid. Even under the FMLA, you would probably need to use all your vacation time and your sick days first before being allowed any unpaid leave.

Can my employer change my job and pay me less because I am pregnant?

Again, this is a complex issue that depends on the individual facts of your case. Whether or not this is pregnancy discrimination depends on what happened to the job and why it the change was made.

There is an old employment law case where a manufacturer would routinely move any pregnant female worker off a certain assembly line because people on that particular line were handling chemicals that were proven to be toxic to the fetuses. Those who worked on this line—both men and women—were paid a lot of money to be exposed to this chemical. However, it was the only area of the plant where a woman could make so much money. An EEOC complaint was filed, and the case went to court. The court found that the employer could legally move the woman away from the toxic chemicals to protect her. However, the employer was required to keep the woman at the same high pay rate until she was no longer pregnant.

In this case the court found that the employer could change a pregnant woman's job due to imminent danger. These are rare events. The more common issue comes when the woman attempts to return to her job only to be told that the job she previously held no longer exists, and that if she wants to work for the company she may need to take a lower-paying job.

There is no easy answer to this type of situation, and it really depends on the employer. If the employer legitimately eliminated the job due to business reasons, it probably would not be considered pregnancy discrimination. This is another situation where you may need to file an EEOC complaint and let the court look at the evidence.

My employer has cut my hours and pay since I revealed that I was pregnant. Is this legal?

If other employees have also had their hours or pay cut, this action by your employer may not be considered specifically pregnancy discrimination. If your employer is in the middle of a downsizing or a business alteration and all employees are being affected, then this is probably not pregnancy discrimination. On the other hand, if you are the only one who has had your hours and pay cut, you might have a discrimination case. To be sure either way, contact a local employment attorney.

FAMILY RESPONSIBILITY AND CAREGIVER DISCRIMINATION

What is family responsibility or caregiver discrimination?

In 2007, the EEOC carved out a niche under Title VII of the Civil Rights Act of 1964 and the Americans with Disabilities Act of 1990 that offers some protection to an employee who either has caregiver responsibilities or who is assumed to have this responsibility due to his or her sex. This is not a new protected category or discrimination basis; it is an interpretation of existing bases of sex discrimination and disability discrimination.

What does this new interpretation of the existing laws do?

This new interpretation of the laws prohibits unlawful disparate treatment of caregivers, no matter what sex the caregiver is.

Some examples of this are:

- not hiring a qualified female applicant because it is assumed she will be the one to care for her children;

- not hiring a young, qualified female because of the false assumption that all women will eventually have children and leave their jobs;

- not putting a qualified female with children into a training or mentoring program because it is assumed she will have more absences in order to take care of the children;

- in a company where time off for child care is given, denying time off for child care to an employee because he is male, under the assumption that men do not care for children;

- denying a single father a part-time position because they are only given to females with children;

- giving promotions to women without children or fathers with stay-at-home wives, rather than the more qualified single women who have children;

- providing flexible schedules for all employees except those with child care responsibilities, and making those who care for children take time off without pay or use their vacation time; and,

- harassing or penalizing workers who take time off to care for aging parents or sick spouses or partners, but allowing parents with children to take time off without issue.

Does that make the caregiver or parent a new protected class with the EEOC?

No. The EEOC enforced laws do not prohibit discrimination based solely on parental or caregiver status. Under the law there still must be a link to a recognized status such as sex or race. This niche fits within the current laws against sex discrimination. The EEOC issued these new guidelines due to the increase in the number of people who are projected to become caregivers of aged parents and due to the long-standing discrimination against women of child-bearing age.

Where can I get more information on caregiver discrimination?

There are two good websites where you can find out more information on caregiver discrimination: **www.worklifelaw.org** and **www. eeoc.gov/policy/docs/caregiving.html**.

Note: This chapter only contains a brief overview of the major discrimination bases. Because laws are always changing some of the above discrimination bases may be limited or expanded by the time this book is published. Your state laws or even the federal laws may have additional bases of discrimination included by the time you read this book. As always you are encouraged to get the current information from reliable Internet sources, such as the EEOC and your local employment attorney.

Chapter 9

OTHER EMPLOYMENT ISSUES

- Are there any protections for injured members of the military who want to go back to work?
- Can an employer give preference in hiring to a veteran with a service-connected disability over other applicants?
- I am an independent contractor. I contract with employers to do certain computer installations. What do I do when a client refuses to follow its part of the agreement, such as providing me with the proper equipment or paying my bills after the work has been completed?
- My former boss is telling everyone lies about me, my work, and my personal life. Not only is this keeping me from being hired at a new company, but it is causing problems at my church. What can I do about this?
- Other than the federal laws discussed in this book, are employees entitled to any additional rights, and where can I locate information on them?

Are there any protections for injured members of the military who want to go back to work?

In addition to injured military covered by the Americans with Disabilities Act (ADA) that is enforced by the EEOC, all members of the military are covered by the Uniformed Services Employment and Reemployment Rights Act (USERRA), which is enforced by the Department of Labor. The USERRA prohibits employers from discriminating against employees due to their military status or military obligations.

Both of these laws require that employers provide *reasonable accommodations* to employees. The USERRA takes the ADA further by requiring employers to make reasonable efforts to aid the injured military person who is returning to a job he or she cannot physically do anymore because of his or her injuries. Some courts have interpreted this to mean that employers should provide accommodations, such as training for other jobs, retraining for the job that was left, a restructuring of that job to meet the abilities of the serviceperson, and other accommodations that go beyond what the ADA requires.

For more information on USERRA and how it is enforced go to **www.dol.gov/vets**.

Can an employer give preference in hiring to a veteran with a service-connected disability over other applicants?

Yes. While the ADA prohibits discrimination against qualified people with disabilities, it does not prevent an employer from having a preference for one potential employee over another. In fact, the U.S. government—in coordination with several veteran organizations—actively encourages employers to make room for one of the many veterans who were injured while serving the country. There are specific rules and regulations that govern hiring veterans by federal employers and detail what is considered a veteran's preference, which is given to all veterans, including those who are disabled.

For more information on the federal program look at OPM's "Vet Guide" at **www.opm.gov/veterans/html/vetguide.asp** and the OPM's Disabled Veterans Affirmative Action Program at **www. opm.gov/veterans/dvaap.asp**.

I am an independent contractor. I contract with employers to do certain computer installations. What do I do when a client refuses to follow its part of the agreement, such as providing me with the proper equipment or paying my bills after the work has been completed?

Because you are not an employee, most of the employment laws discussed in this book will not apply to you. If your client will not adhere to a written contract that he or she has signed, you may ultimately need to sue the client in a local civil court on the issue of breach of contract.

Before you start a court fight, you should find out if the client has a problem with the services that you performed. If the issue is merely that the client feels something is still in error on your project, it may be cheaper for you to fix the problem in order to get your money. If the issue is that the client did not provide you with the proper equipment, perhaps the manufacturer is the problem or there is just a misunderstanding.

If the problem is not something that you can fix, you may want to send a certified letter to the client reminding him or her of the obligations under the contract that he or she signed, and giving a deadline to either follow the terms of the contract or deal with your attorney. You might then want to find a local attorney who handles contract breach litigation in your local court.

Many independent contractors who use contracts with clients make the mistake of not putting provisions into the contract for client problems, such as nonpayment. In order to protect yourself, these items must be addressed in accordance with your local laws.

The following are some examples of issues that should be addressed in an independent contractor's agreement with their client.

- Each contract should be specifically tailored to detail what both the client and what the independent contractor are required to supply and the date these items will be available. There should also be some direction as to what will happen and who will be financially liable if these items are not ready on time.

- Each contract should list exactly what the independent contractor is to do in detail. This should include the goals of the project according to the client, how the client will measure or determine that the project is complete, and how the client intends to determine if the project is a success.

- Each contract should specify who will sign off on the project for the client and what steps will be taken if the client refuses to sign off. An independent contractor does not want to spend the rest of his or her career working for one very picky client who refuses to pay the independent contractor, so this must be very detailed. Some contracts may contain a clause that requires professional arbitration for disagreements that cannot be resolved in a short period of time.

- Each contract should detail the hours the independent contractor will work, location, and what happens when the contractor needs time off.

- Each contract should specify the amount of payment and how it is calculated. There should be provisions for late payments and nonpayment. Late payments may include a grace period and an interest percentage (to be exercised at the option of the independent contractor), which is added to the owed amount. For issues of nonpayment, there should be an indication that the independent contractor has the option to take the matter to court and go after the money owed, interest on that money, and the contractor's attorney fees.

My former boss is telling everyone lies about me, my work, and my personal life. Not only is this keeping me from being hired at a new company, but it is causing problems at my church. What can I do about this?

If your former employer is spreading lies about you, you may be able to file a defamation lawsuit against him or her. It really depends on the specific laws in your state. Some states allow an employer to say whatever it wants to about a former employee, as long as what the employer actually believes what it's saying. However, this is the law in the minority of states. Most states limit what a former employer can say about an employee to the date the employee was hired, the date the employee and employer separated, and in some states, the employee's salary range and rehire rights.

If you live in the majority of states, you may be able to file a civil suit against your employer. However, defamation cases can be complex case and should be handled by a local attorney. In some cases the employee needs to present a potential employer as a witness who will testify under oath that had it not been for the poor recommendation from the former employer, he or she would have hired you. Unfortunately, many employers do not want to get involved with a court action for a person who is not an employee and who has the courage to take issues to court.

Another complex issue is showing damages. If the problem with your church is that a few people made fun of you, it is doubtful that would rise to the level of damages a court looks for. On the other hand, if the church demoted you from a position of power or a paid position, that may be evidence against your former employer. Again, this is not an easy case and needs the assistance of a local attorney who is familiar with your state's laws.

Other than the federal laws discussed in this book, are employees entitled to any additional rights, and where can I locate information on them?

The laws discussed in this book are the ones most commonly referenced in employment legal complaints. However, there are many other laws that apply to employees. To find these other laws, the first place to look is at the laws in the state where you live. Your state can have many additional laws and assistance for employees. For your convenience we have compiled information by state in Appendices A, B, C, and D in the back of this book. Appendix E also has addresses of many websites that contain additional information on employee rights that you might find useful.

If you need more information, go to your state's primary website— each state has one. You may also want to go to the Department of Labor's primary website at **www.dol.gov** to access information on the many agencies that report to the Department of Labor.

As for your state's actual laws, most state statutes are on the Internet. You may need to do an Internet search to find them. If you prefer a written book, many local libraries have the local laws printed out. You may also want to look at the law libraries contained in most courthouses and in law schools. Finally, if you still cannot find the information, you may want to contact a local attorney for his or her assistance.

Section IV:
Getting Relief

This section details the types of relief an employee may be able to obtain for various employment law violations by his or her employer. Chapter 10 discusses the usual steps for filing a complaint. This chapter gives tips on dealing with the agencies and what to expect from them. Chapter 11 talks about actually going to court against your employer. Chapter 12 details how to obtain unemployment benefits and what to expect from that agency. Finally, Chapters 13 and 14 give overviews of workers' compensation claims and the FMLA.

Chapter 10

FILING COMPLAINTS

EEOC

- How do I file an EEOC complaint?
- What about EEOC complaints filed by my attorney?
- What type of information does the EEOC want from me?
- What happens after the EEOC complaint is filed at the EEOC district office?
- I filed my own case with the EEOC almost a year ago, and it was assigned to an investigator. The investigator has been working on this case, but it is taking a long time. Can I get an attorney to push this case along?
- What is a right to sue letter, and how can I use it?
- Can I take my case into the federal district court without an attorney?
- Why won't the EEOC represent me in court?

Local Human Rights Departments

- Are all state offices that take workplace discrimination complaints called human rights departments?
- How can I find out if my state has a facility like a human rights department or agency where I can file an employment discrimination case?
- What can my local or state's human rights department do for employees?
- What happens in a state's or local human rights department complaint?
- Why would I want to file a complaint with a human rights department rather than the EEOC?
- What are the downsides for using the state agency?

Department of Labor (DOL)

- What does the DOL do for employees?
- When should a complaint be filed with the DOL?

- What is the difference between the federal DOL and a state's DOL?
- How do I file a complaint with the DOL?
- My employer has refused to pay overtime to all employees in all of its nationwide offices, due to a classification error. Who can I turn to for help in getting overtime pay?
- I was let go from my sales position. According to my records, I am still owed several thousands of dollars in both commissions and bonuses. What can I do?
- Can my employer hold my last paycheck when I am terminated in order to get his stuff back?

NLRB
- What is the NLRB?
- How do I file a complaint with the NLRB?
- The union that I have been a member of for the last twenty years is ignoring my complaint that I am being forced out of my job due to my age. I have already filed an EEOC complaint against my employer. Can I file any complaints against my union?

EEOC

How do I file an EEOC complaint?

First, you need to find the appropriate EEOC office for your complaint. Go to the website **www.eeoc.gov/offices.html**, and select your state to find the appropriate office for your complaint. Click on the page for that individual office. Each district office has its own webpage. On that page you will find information on the jurisdictional area of that office. *Jurisdictional area* is the state, county, or city where the incident of employment discrimination took place.

Then, you need to follow the directions to file your complaint. Each EEOC district office has detailed instructions on how it wants a discrimination complaint to be filed, and each has its own procedures that you must follow. Some offices will ask you to call and make an appointment to speak with an intake or investigation person. Other offices will accept a filled-out form that you can download from the Internet.

What about EEOC complaints filed by my attorney?

Your attorney will obtain the proper EEOC form and may add a legal brief to the form. You will need to sign the document just as you would if you had filled out the form with the assistance of an EEOC intake person. As we have said in previous chapters, the primary reason for having an attorney at the filing point is to make sure that you file every claim that you are entitled to.

What type of information does the EEOC want from me?

Generally, you will be asked for your name, address, and phone number, and the name, address, and phone number of your employer. You will also need to provide the dates that the discrimination occurred and what type of discrimination it was. You need to remember two things here:

1. there are time limits for reporting discrimination. In most cases the time limit is three hundred days, so an incident that happened two years ago will probably not help in your complaint; and,

2. you are limited to filing a complaint about the discrimination due to age, race, sex, color, national origin, religion, disability, and retaliation. The EEOC office will ask you to state that you want to file a discrimination charge and sign the document.

The EEOC district office where you are filing the charge may want additional information. Also your attorney will provide a lot of additional information in his or her written complaint for your case.

What happens after the EEOC complaint is filed at the EEOC district office?

Generally these are the steps an EEOC complaint will follow:

1. The written complaint will be reviewed to see if it is within the correct geographic area, was filed within the time limits that the EEOC has set up, and is a complaint about a violation of a discrimination law that the EEOC enforces. If the complaint does not meet these requirements, it will probably be immediately rejected by the EEOC.

2. If the complaint is accepted, it will be assigned a case number. At any time in this process, once this number is assigned, the employee can ask to have the case dismissed with a right to sue letter, and then the employee and his or her attorney can file the complaint in a federal district court for trial.

3. Some EEOC district offices offer access to the mediation program at this point. If either party has requested mediation, this is the point at which arrangements for the mediation will be made. Mediation only proceeds if both parties agree to it. If mediation is successful, the parties settle the case and the complaint is withdrawn.

4. If mediation is not used or is unsuccessful, an EEOC investigator is assigned to the complaint. Depending on that investigator's

workload the complaint may be worked on immediately or handled in the order it was received.

5. The investigator will contact both parties and any witnesses provided by the parties. The investigator may request documents or meet face-to-face with the parties. In some instances, the investigator may do a walkthrough of the employer's facility.

6. The investigator will work with both parties to reach a mutually agreeable settlement. If a settlement is agreed to, the investigator will file the proper paperwork to dismiss the complaint and will assist the parties should problems arise with the settlement.

7. If no settlement is reached, once the investigator has completed the investigation, he or she will write up a decision. In very rare cases, the EEOC will take on the case and proceed to court. Otherwise, the employee will get a decision from the EEOC. Most decisions include a *right to sue letter*, which gives the employee ninety days to file his or her complaint in the federal district court for a formal trial.

I filed my own case with the EEOC almost a year ago, and it was assigned to an investigator. The investigator has been working on this case, but it is taking a long time. Can I get an attorney to push this case along?

It is doubtful than an attorney can do anything to move your case along any faster. As long as your investigator is still with the EEOC and contacts you periodically, you know the agency is continuing to work on your case.

EEOC investigators carry a huge workload of cases. Much of the investigation consists of waiting—they call the employer or employee and wait for a return call; they request documents and wait to get them; they request a witness list from the employee and wait for that information; they call the witnesses and wait for a call back; if one side offers a settlement, they call the other side and wait for a response. The job of EEOC investigator is not easy, especially when balancing the number of cases they do.

Your case may be helped by the introduction of an attorney who will work with the investigator, especially if the investigator has been asking you for information that you have been unable to provide, if mediation has been scheduled, or if the employer is willing to enter into a settlement negotiation. On the other hand, an attorney who merely calls the investigator frequently just to ask when the investigation will be finished will hinder the completion of the case, in addition to costing you attorney fees.

The most helpful time to get an attorney involved in an EEOC discrimination case is before you file your complaint with EEOC. An attorney can review the facts of your case and may be able to find additional claims that need to be filed. The attorney can also draft the legal brief and file the complaint with the EEOC. Then the investigator will begin the process by working with this attorney.

What is a right to sue letter, and how can I use it?

A right to sue letter is issued by the EEOC for complaints that it does not intend to represent in court. It is highly unusual for the EEOC to take a case into court. There are three common groups of complaints that will get this letter.

1. Many times the EEOC can get the employer to correct a discrimination problem without the employer admitting any

guilt in the current case. This may protect employees going forward, but does little to resolve the issue with the particular employee that brought the first complaint, unless the employer and employee agree to a settlement.

2. In other complaints, the EEOC investigators cannot find any evidence that there ever was a violation of the discrimination laws. This does not mean that the employee who brought the suit was not discriminated against; it only means that the investigator was unable to find any conclusive proof of discrimination. An employee must remember that the time from the discrimination incident to the point when the investigator looks at the case can be more than one year. In that period of time documents can be lost, witnesses can forget, and the supervisor that caused the initial problem may have moved on to a new company.

3. Finally, there are some cases where an employee filed an EEOC complaint due to an incident that does not violate the discrimination laws that the EEOC enforces or, upon investigation, does not appear to have happened in the manner that the employee remembers it.

What the right to sue letter says is that the EEOC is not taking this case to court, but if the employee wants to, he or she can pay to have the case taken to trial in the federal district court. It is a trial in every sense and expense. Just filing a case in this court is complex.

Can I take my case into the federal district court without an attorney?
An employee with a right to sue letter can file a case on his or her

own behalf. This is called pro se. As a pro se plaintiff, you may also ask the court to appoint an attorney to your case, after your filing has been accepted by the court and if you can prove an inability to pay.

Remember, one of the most difficult parts of a successful discrimination case is actually filing the case with the court, citing the proper laws, and putting it in the approved format. Only when that is done correctly and is accepted can you apply for an attorney. Most courts require that you prove you are *indigent* or unable to pay. Commonly, this is proven with IRS annual filings or other reports.

Why won't the EEOC represent me in court?

The EEOC takes very, very few cases into court. Just because the EEOC will not represent you in court, though, does not negatively reflect on the merits of your particular case. The EEOC is continually being bombarded with discrimination complaints that need to be processed. As the economy continues to have problems, employers are allowed to send jobs offshore, and stockholders demand that expenses be cut, the complaints to the EEOC continue to rise. The EEOC continues to work at the maximum level with little, if any, additional government funding for all the extra cases it needs to consider.

LOCAL HUMAN RIGHTS DEPARTMENTS

Are all state offices that take workplace discrimination complaints called human rights departments?

No. Human rights departments are actually called different names in different states. Human rights departments are agencies or departments of states that enforce the state discrimination laws. While the official name of the office varies, these offices are places where employees can file discrimination complaints against their employers.

How can I find out if my state has a facility like a human rights department or agency where I can file an employment discrimination case?

Appendix A contains a list of all state agencies that handle discrimination complaints, so you can start there.

Another way to get to your state's agency that handles workplace discrimination is to go to your state's official website. From that website, you should be able to link to information for employees or workers and find out more information on discrimination laws in your state.

What can my local or state's human rights department do for employees?

The local or state's human rights department enforces discrimination laws. The laws that they enforce are those written by the state or city. These discrimination laws may mirror the laws that the EEOC enforces, or they may add more bases of discrimination. Filing a complaint with a local or state agency will allow you to use the state or local court system if the case cannot be settled at the agency level.

What happens in a state's or local human rights department complaint?

A complaint filed in a state or local human rights department will be handled similarly to the way that the EEOC handles complaints. Once the complaint is accepted and assigned a case number, notice of the complaint is sent to the employer for a required response. The case then goes into a database awaiting an available investigator.

In states where the activity in the human rights department is low, the investigator may be assigned even before the employer's response is sent in. For those offices that have backlogs, it can take several months to a year before an investigator is assigned. Please note several of the states that carry a huge backlog have a time limit on how long the case can sit waiting for an investigator to be assigned. Once that time limit is reached, you may be given the option to go into a higher (more expensive and more time consuming) court or have the case dismissed (without being able to reinstate it).

Once an investigator is assigned, he or she will contact both the employer and the employee for additional information. The investigator may hold a fact-finding hearing and assist in settlement negotiations. When the investigator is sure that all the investigation is completed, he or she will write up a decision and send that decision to a supervisor. The decision will either be that the investigator did not find sufficient evidence of discrimination or that the case has merit and should go on to the next higher level.

Many times, if the investigator finds that the case has merit, the case will be settled because the employer does not want the complaint to proceed to a more expensive, more time-consuming court. If there is no settlement offered, the employee may need to consider whether the extra expense and time to take his or her complaint to the next level is worth it. This entire process may take more than a year.

Why would I want to file a complaint with a human rights department rather than the EEOC?

If your state's human rights agency enforces laws that include more bases of discrimination in their statutes that affect your case, you may want to use the state agency. For example, many states are adding sexual orientation as a basis of discrimination to state laws, while it is still not included in the laws that the EEOC enforces.

If your state agency can process a discrimination complaint quicker than it takes for your local EEOC office, you may want to file with the state agency. If you are sure that you want to pursue the complaint in the state court system instead of the federal court system, you may want to file your complaint with the state agency. You can always elect to file with the state agency but also do a dual filing with the EEOC.

Remember that the time limits for the state's human rights agency may differ from that of the EEOC. If you are only filing with the state agency, or are filing with both the state and the EEOC, you will need to adhere to the state deadlines.

What are the downsides for using the state agency?

Right now, both the EEOC and the state agencies are being over-loaded with discrimination complaints. While some states have certain mechanisms to handle the increased number of complaints, those mechanisms may result in cases not getting the attention they deserve.

In this poor economic climate for employees, as the number of complaints increase, the amount of money that is budgeted for this in the state department is going down. Many of the state agencies are caught in a situation where they cannot hire additional personnel to handle the increased number of complaints, while at the same time they are required by law to process all complaints within a specified time period.

Some states have attempted to resolve this problem by completely eliminating the constraints on the length of time that a complaint will remain in the agency. In those states, your complaint may be in the agency for a long period of time. In other state agencies, discrimination complaints are heavily scrutinized when they are initially filed to weed out those cases that probably are not violations of discrimination laws. This may not give a discrimination complaint the scrutiny it needs, which makes it even more important to have an attorney draft your discrimination complaint. For other states, the length of time the state can hold the complaint remains the same, but once that time is up, the complaint will be dismissed.

DEPARTMENT OF LABOR (DOL)

What does the DOL do for employees?

The Department of Labor oversees almost every aspect of labor laws in the United States. The Department of Labor has a very informative website explaining what it does, which you can visit at **www.dol.gov**. At this website, an employee can obtain information on wages and work hours, workplace safety and health, retirement and health benefits, disability resources, information for job seekers, resources for people who have been laid off, and training.

When should a complaint be filed with the DOL?

The Department of Labor oversees many government agencies that have to deal with workplace issues. Generally, when an employee has questions or wishes to file a complaint against his or her employer regarding wages, commissions, bonuses, or overtime, the Department of Labor is the place to go.

Other agencies that come under the DOL include:

• Bureau of International Labor Affairs;

• Center for Faith-Based and Community Initiatives;

- Employee Benefits Security Administration;

- Employment Standard Administration;

- Employment and Training Administration;

- Energy Employees Occupational Illness Compensation Program;

- Mine Safety and Health Administration;

- Occupational Safety and Health Administration (OSHA);

- Office of Disability Employment Policy;

- Office of Federal Contract Compliance Program;

- Office of Labor-Management Standards;

- Office of Workers' Compensation Programs (OWCP);

- Veterans' Employment and Training Service;

- Wage and Hour Division; and,

- Women's Bureau.

The DOL enforces any laws enacted by these agencies. For example, if you file an OSHA complaint against your employer, the DOL will be the agency that reviews the complaint and decides if the employer is in violation of that OSHA law. This is a very simplistic view of the DOL. Remember that the DOL has multiple layers of administrative rules and procedures in addition to the rules and procedures of the agencies that it oversees.

What is the difference between the federal DOL and a state's DOL?

Much like the EEOC, the federal DOL enforces the labor laws that are enacted by the federal government and apply to all states. The state's Department of Labor will enforce those state laws.

State Department of Labor offices can vary in what they do. In a large state that has many of its own laws, the state DOL can have its hands full just enforcing the state's labor laws. In other states, the state DOL office can range from merely a conduit that assists workers in obtaining benefits from other departments, to an all-in-one department that handles all employee-employer issues.

Appendix B is a list of the various Department of Labor offices for each state.

How do I file a complaint with the DOL?

For both state and federal Department of Labor complaints, go to the website and download the proper form or contact the office to have that form sent to you. Fill out the form, attach copies of any evidence you may have, and follow the directions about processing your complaint.

Once the complaint is accepted, you will be contacted by someone at the DOL office that you filed the complaint with.

My employer has refused to pay overtime to all employees in all of its nationwide offices, due to a classification error. Who can I turn to for help in getting overtime pay?

If your employer is refusing to pay overtime to its employees, the Department of Labor will initiate an investigation through its Wage and Hour Division. If the investigation shows that the employer has violated the Federal Labor Standards Act (FLSA) by misclassifying you as exempt from the FLSA requirements, the DOL can get you and the other employees back overtime pay.

I was let go from my sales position. According to my records, I am still owed several thousands of dollars in both commissions and bonuses. What can I do?

You will need to file a complaint with the Department of Labor for the commissions and bonuses owed to you. You will be asked to fill out a form and to provide copies of any documents—such as an agreement about commissions and bonuses from your employer—information from the employee manual about these issues, proof that you made sales that would result in commissions, and any other documentation that shows you are owed these amounts. Do not send original evidentiary documents unless specifically asked to. Keep a copy of the complaint form with all evidence for your records.

Can my employer hold my last paycheck when I am terminated in order to get his stuff back?

Holding onto salary that you have already earned is a violation of the federal minimum-wage laws, and you can file a complaint with the Department of Labor for such action. However, based on court rulings, it does appear to be lawful for an employer to hold back vacation pay in order to get the employer's property back. The employer would need to state this in its policy or rules manual.

NLRB

What is the NLRB?

The National Labor Relations Board (NLRB) is a federal agency that enforces the National Labor Relations Act, which is the primary act that governs the relationship between unions and employees, and unions and employers. In general terms, this law guarantees the rights of employees to organize as a union, to let the union enter into collective bargaining on behalf of the employees, and to allow the union to represent the employees along certain guidelines.

The goal of the NLRB is to:

- protect workers who form, join, support, or assist unions;

- protect workers who—as a group, without a union—engage in protected concerted activities to modify wages or working conditions;

- protect workers from discrimination based on union-related activities; and,

- protect workers from unfair labor practices initiated by the union.

How do I file a complaint with the NLRB?

Start at the National Labor Relations Board's website, **www.nlrb. gov.** Locate the NLRB regional office closest to your workplace. Download the appropriate form, fill it out, and file it with that regional office.

There are only two forms that you potentially need to fill out. One is for filing charges against your employer and the other is for filing charges against your union. Some regional offices also require you to take additional steps prior to filing these forms, so make sure you read and follow them carefully.

The union that I have been a member of for the last twenty years is ignoring my complaint that I am being forced out of my job due to my age. I have already filed an EEOC complaint against my employer. Can I file any complaints against my union?

Complaints against unions for lack of representation or discrimination in representation should be filed with the National Labor Relations Board. Once you file the complaint with the regional office, someone there will investigate your accusations and get back to you. The regional NLRB office may also assist you in obtaining a settlement with the union.

Chapter 11

GOING TO TRIAL

- How much money can I get if I sue my employer?
- Can the court force my employer to rehire me?
- What is a class-action employment suit?
- How can I get the EEOC to sue my employer on my behalf?
- What types of courts do employment cases go to?
- How much will my attorney charge to take my case into court?
- Why do employment law cases take so long to get to trial?
- What is pain and suffering?
- What is a deposition?
- Why are my witnesses refusing to back me up?
- My employer is lying to the court. What can I do? My employer has forged documents with a signature that is not mine. How can I prove this?

How much money can I get if I sue my employer?

If your EEOC case proceeds into federal district court, you will be able to ask for more money than in a settlement at the agency level because at this level you can ask for compensation for pain and suffering. Each case is different and must be individually evaluated by an employment attorney who is experienced in going to federal district court. Of course, going into federal district court will cost the employee more in expenses.

Can the court force my employer to rehire me?

While the court may be able to force your employer to rehire you, it may not be in your best interest to return to work for the employer that discriminated against you and that you filed a lawsuit against. In the rare cases where an employee does return to work, that employee may be subjected to treatment that is not a violation of the law but that makes working conditions difficult. Before deciding to ask the court to force you to be rehired or accepting a rehire, consult with an employment attorney.

There are some laws that are enforced by the Department of Labor that require that the employer rehire the employee and provide back pay plus interest if the employer is found guilty of a legal violation. While the court cannot demand that the employee and employer give up their free will through a rehire, it is a method to resolve the litigation or at least minimize the amount of back pay the employer is responsible for in the case of an appeal. If the trial court orders the employer to rehire and the employer refuses, then the employer continues to be responsible for an accumulating amount of back pay while the case goes to appeal. If it is the employee who refuses to return to work for this employer, then the back pay amount stops accumulating at that point, even though the case can continue on appeal.

What is a class-action employment suit?

A class-action lawsuit is where one attorney represents a group of clients against a defendant because of the same violation. Class-action cases are not handled by every attorney; it is a unique practice area with special procedural requirements. The EEOC will sometimes file a class-action suit, representing many employees who previously filed EEOC complaints against an employer.

How can I get the EEOC to sue my employer on my behalf?

You cannot make the EEOC sue your employer on your behalf. The EEOC investigators will evaluate your case under the same guidelines as all others are evaluated. The EEOC selects very few cases to sue for the employee. There are no magic words that will put your case in this group. Usually, it takes several EEOC complaints to be filed against one employer before the EEOC steps in and files a case against that employer. Those cases are class actions, which usually result in not only solving the employer's discrimination problem, but in most instances providing a financial settlement for all employees in the class.

What types of courts do employment cases go to?

If a case has gone through the EEOC complaint process, it will go into the federal district court closest to you. Department of Labor cases can go into federal administrative courts. Government employee complaints are appealed to the Merit Systems Protection Board, which holds an administrative trial and can go into the state federal court system. Unemployment benefits cases can end up in a local county civil court. As for the states, each state sets the path that cases go on during an appeal. Some agencies have their own administrative courts and may allow cases to proceed into state civil courts.

How much will my attorney charge to take my case into court?

The answer to this question depends on the attorney and your case. Remember, for every case that proceeds into court, there are significant expenses before the trial ever begins. These are expenses for things like deposition costs, filing fees, and investigator fees. Some attorneys may take your case on a contingency basis, taking a portion of your settlement if you win, but charging you nothing if you lose your case. Attorneys will usually only take a case on a contingency basis, though, if the attorney believes the case will win and has enough money of his or her own to carry the case through trial. Some attorneys will ask for a certain amount of money up front, and then deduct their expenses from that amount. However, this is an important question for you to ask when interviewing attorneys.

Why do employment law cases take so long to get to trial?

Employment law cases take so long to get to trial because the majority of employment discrimination cases must first be filed with an administrative agency before going to trial. The agency then investigates and attempts to resolve the issue. Only after the administrative agency has made a determination on the case, can it finally go to trial. Again, keep in mind that there are some cases that can go directly into civil court, such as breach of an employment contract. Your attorney can advise you as to what must be done on your case and the approximate time it will take to get through the system. For employment cases that must first go to an agency and then to trial, the time can be measured in years.

What is pain and suffering?

Pain and suffering is the extra emotional stress that plaintiffs claim in some trials, which can potentially cause a higher than normal punitive cost to an employer. An employee will only get damages for pain and suffering if he or she wins the case and the court awards the amount. In the case of an employment discrimination case filed with an agency like the EEOC, all the employee can usually get is a reimbursement for salary lost, benefits lost and paid for by the employee, outstanding expenses that the employer owed the employee, and reimbursement of attorney's fees. Many employees want to go to trial in order to get extra funding and punish the employer for bad treatment.

What is a deposition?

A deposition consists of questions asked by an attorney and answered under oath by a witness or principal in a case, prior to trial. Your attorney will depose your employer, your immediate supervisor, and any potential witnesses. The employer's attorney will depose you and any of your witnesses.

However, some agencies do not allow face-to-face depositions and instead require that all parties use *written interrogatories*. *Written interrogatories* are written questions that must be answered under oath.

Why are my witnesses refusing to back me up?

This is a very common question asked in discrimination complaints. Your witnesses may still be employed by the same employer you are suing. The employer may have made it clear that it will retaliate against anyone who takes your side, or this threat may just be implied. While an agency may provide some protection for these witnesses, if the case goes to trial, then they are not protected. You cannot blame a witness for not wanting to put his or her job on the line, especially in today's economy.

My employer is lying to the court. What can I do? My employer has forged documents with a signature that is not mine. How can I prove this?

Immediately tell your attorney about this. If you can find evidence to prove the lie, provide that to your attorney. If whether or not the signature is genuine is the issue, offer to show something (like an identification card) that has your signature on it, which will show the differences in the signatures. Trust your attorney with these things. An experienced employment attorney will not only not be shocked by the employer's behavior, but will be expecting it.

Chapter 12

OBTAINING UNEMPLOYMENT BENEFITS

- Can I get unemployment benefits if I quit my job?
- What would I need to do to quit due to a medical need and still potentially receive unemployment benefits?
- If I accuse my boss of sexual harassment, can I then quit and get unemployment benefits?
- My boss is fighting my request for unemployment benefits. He says that I committed misconduct, but I was told that I was fired due to a reduction in staff. What does this mean?
- I was fired for extreme absenteeism. Will I be able to get unemployment benefits?
- I was fired for sexually harassing a co-worker, and I have been told that I will not be able to get unemployment benefits. What if I am innocent of the sexual harassment?
- I was turned down for unemployment benefits because my employer said I was fired due to misconduct. I applied for an appeal and received a telephone hearing. Is the telephone hearing legal?
- Do I need a lawyer at a telephone hearing for unemployment benefits?
- What goes on at a telephone hearing for unemployment benefits?
- Do unemployment benefits hearings always take place over the phone?
- I won my telephone hearing, but my employer is now appealing that decision. What does this mean?
- I lost my telephone appeal hearing last month. Today I found written evidence that supports my case. Can I provide that to the Board of Review or to anyone in the state's unemployment administration?

Can I get unemployment benefits if I quit my job?

Usually, if you quit your job, you will not qualify for unemployment benefits. However, there are two exceptions to this rule. If you quit due to a legitimate medical need, which is supported by your doctor, or you quit due to sexual harassment that the employer refuses to stop, then you may be able to receive unemployment benefits anyway.

What would I need to do to quit due to a medical need and still potentially receive unemployment benefits?

First, you would need to be under the care of a licensed physician. The physician would need to diagnose your medical problem as something being caused directly by your job. You would need to present these findings to your employer. Your employer would then get an opportunity to move you to another location or eliminate the item making you ill. Your doctor would need to order you, in writing, to terminate your job for your health.

If I accuse my boss of sexual harassment, can I then quit and get unemployment benefits?

If someone at your job has been sexually harassing you, you must go through the proper channels to report the offender. Most often you will find a procedure for reporting sexual harassment in your employee manual. Reporting generally means that you must notify your supervisor, manager, or even higher-up management in addition to the human resources department. Once notified, you must give the employer sufficient time to conduct an investigation of your complaint. Each instance of sexual harassment must be reported in this manner.

If your employer is unable or unwilling to stop the sexual harassment or relocate you to a place where you will not be subject to this behavior, then you may consider quitting due to sexual harassment. If you do quit, make sure that you have notified your employer in writing that you are leaving the company due to the sexual harassment and its inability or unwillingness to put a stop to it.

My boss is fighting my request for unemployment benefits. He says that I committed misconduct, but I was told that I was fired due to a reduction in staff. What does this mean?

When a former employee applies for unemployment benefits, a notice is sent to the former employer. If the employer wants the state to deny the employee these benefits, all the employer needs to do is check a box that indicates "misconduct" or "employee quit" and sign a form. Many employers (close to 90%) decide to try to deny former employees unemployment benefits because there is a financial cost to the employer. However, the ultimate decision-maker of who gets benefits is the state department that issues unemployment benefits.

For a state department, the word "misconduct" has a certain legal meaning. While the employer may look at the word as a description of an employee who goofed off, talked back, or made errors, the word actually means something very different. Under the rules for unemployment, misconduct means that the employer had a rule or policy, the rule or policy was something that was a serious issue affecting the bottom line or safety of other employees, the employee violated that rule or policy, the employee was warned that if he or she violated that rule or policy again he or she would be terminated, and the employee willfully and deliberately violated the rule or policy.

This legal definition of misconduct can be beneficial to the employee's attorney in obtaining unemployment benefits. Employers rarely understand what misconduct really means in this context.

I was fired for extreme absenteeism. Will I be able to get unemployment benefits?

You probably will not be able to collect unemployment benefits. The courts have determined that an employer has a legitimate right to require employees to report to work every day that they are assigned, report to work on time, and stay for the full time of their shift, even if that is not listed as a specific company rule or policy. Attendance or absenteeism is considered to be a very important requirement of employment that not only affects the employer's bottom line, but the environment for all other employees. Even if the employer does not protest the former employee's application for unemployment benefits, the state department that administers these benefits usually will not allow a person who was fired due to extreme absenteeism to obtain unemployment benefits.

I was fired for sexually harassing a co-worker, and I have been told that I will not be able to get unemployment benefits. What if I am innocent of the sexual harassment?

You probably will still not be able to obtain unemployment benefits. Like being terminated for absenteeism, being terminated due to an accusation of sexual harassment has been considered by the courts as a legitimate reason to deny unemployment benefits because of its importance and implications to other employees' safety. In the majority of these cases, the employer has a sexual harassment policy. That policy usually allows for an investigation and possible termination. If an employer exercises its option to terminate the person accused of sexual harassment, the employer has fulfilled its duties and can legitimately cite misconduct.

As for being innocent of the sexual harassment charge, that does not play into the decision from the state's unemployment office. The office only looks at whether or not the employer followed its own policy and that the termination was due to the accusation.

I was turned down for unemployment benefits because my employer said I was fired due to misconduct. I applied for an appeal and received a telephone hearing. Is the telephone hearing legal?

Yes, the telephone hearing is legal and is the most important part of trying to obtain unemployment benefits when your former employer protests. The person running the telephone appeal is an administrative law judge, sometimes called a referee. That person has the power of a judge whom you see in a regular courtroom. The evidence and testimony that is presented at this telephone hearing should be your entire case, just as if you went to court in person. Anything not presented or not said at this hearing will be barred.

Do I need a lawyer at a telephone hearing for unemployment benefits?

Yes, you should have a lawyer representing you during a telephone hearing for unemployment benefits. The telephone hearing is your final opportunity to present your case for receiving unemployment benefits. It is run by an administrative law judge using the same procedural rules as any trial. Your employer will probably have an attorney. Unless you are familiar with court procedure and the laws that apply to obtaining unemployment benefits, you will need an attorney.

What goes on at a telephone hearing for unemployment benefits?

Before your telephone hearing, your attorney will speak with you regarding the details of you leaving your job. Your attorney will then provide you with a strategy, including what will be asked at the hearing and the arguments that will be used on your behalf. Prior to the telephone hearing, discovery documents and evidence will be shared with the opponent and the administrative law judge. The administrative law judge will get all parties, their attorneys, and their witnesses on a conference call. Attorneys may be allowed to make opening statements. The judge will ask you and the employer questions, and then allow the attorneys to ask questions of their clients and cross-examine the other side. Attorneys will then make their closing statements.

Do unemployment benefits hearings always take place over the phone?

No. In many parts of the country, administrative judges prefer to have hearings in person. Everything runs the same in an in-person administrative hearing as it does over the telephone, but instead of being on a conference call, everyone is present in the same room.

I won my telephone hearing, but my employer is now appealing that decision. What does this mean?

After the administrative law judge makes a decision on your unemployment benefits case, the employee and the employer have thirty days to appeal the decision to a Board of Review. This appeal is done by presenting a written legal brief, which argues one side of the case and cites both past cases and laws that support the arguments.

I lost my telephone appeal hearing last month. Today I found written evidence that supports my case. Can I provide that to the Board of Review or to anyone in the state's unemployment administration?

No, unfortunately that late evidence cannot be presented. Your final opportunity to present evidence was the telephone appeal hearing, and all evidence had to be presented there. A brief to the Board of Review cannot add any new evidence other than what was already stated at the appeal hearing.

Chapter 13

WORKERS' COMPENSATION

- What is workers' compensation?
- I caused the incident that injured me at work. Do I still qualify for workers' compensation?
- Are all employees covered by workers' compensation if they need it?
- What type of medical care will workers' compensation pay for?
- What do I do if I get injured on the job?
- What can I do if my employer refuses to file a workers' compensation claim with its insurance company for an on-the-job injury?
- When do I need to get an attorney for a workers' compensation claim? What if I cannot afford to hire an attorney?
- Can my employer require that I see two or three of its doctors in a workers' compensation claim?
- I was injured on the job and now am under medical care with restrictions. Does my employer have to provide light-duty work for me?
- My boss is threatening to terminate me for excessive absenteeism even though I have a workers' comp injury. Can he do this?

What is workers' compensation?

Workers' compensation is a system of benefits provided by state laws to most workers who get injured while on the job.

Go to Appendix D for a list of the Workers' Compensation Commissions in your state, along with information about filing workers' comp claims in your state.

I caused the incident that injured me at work. Do I still qualify for workers' compensation?

Yes. The laws that govern the workers' compensation benefits are not concerned with fault. If the worker is injured on the job, he or she probably does qualify for the benefits.

Are all employees covered by workers' compensation if they need it?

Almost every person who is considered an employee will qualify for workers' compensation if injured on the job. However, it is up to individual states to determine eligibility. For the majority of states, the employer is required by law to obtain workers' compensation insurance and continue to pay premiums for this policy.

What type of medical care will workers' compensation pay for?

Most workers' compensation polices will pay for reasonable medical care, temporary total disability, vocational rehabilitation, permanent disability, and death benefits. Again, because this is required by state laws, each state may have different requirements.

What do I do if I get injured on the job?

You should report the injury to your employer so that your employer can file a workers' compensation claim with its insurance carrier. Your state may have a time limit—such as thirty days from the date of the injury—for you to report the injury to your employer. Usually you will need to provide the date and place of the accident and a description of the accident and injury. In order to protect yourself, you should give your written report to your manager and keep a copy of it for yourself.

What can I do if my employer refuses to file a workers' compensation claim with its insurance company for an on-the-job injury?

Most states require that all workers' comp injuries be handled by filing a claim with the workers' compensation insurance carrier. If your employer does not have workers' compensation insurance, it may be in violation of state law and you could go to your state's workers' compensation commission. You may want to hire a workers' compensation attorney to assist you if you find yourself in this situation.

When do I need to get an attorney for a workers' compensation claim? What if I cannot afford to hire an attorney?

If you are having problems obtaining financial assistance for a workers' comp injury, or if your employer refuses to even acknowledge the injury, it is best to hire a workers' compensation attorney to assist you. The attorney can file a workers' compensation action with the state's commission. That commission has the power to award settlements in the case.

As for attorney fees, a workers' compensation attorney does not make a lot of money from his or her clients, which is why most workers' comp attorneys do a large volume of these cases. The law limits what amount a workers' comp attorney can charge. Most states limit this to a small percentage of the compensation that the employee would get in a workers' compensation lawsuit.

Can my employer require that I see two or three of its doctors in a workers' compensation claim?

In most states the employer can require that the employee get examined by the employer's own medical personnel. This is especially true in a soft tissue injury where there are no broken bones or obvious injuries.

I was injured on the job and now am under medical care with restrictions. Does my employer have to provide light-duty work for me?

Neither the Workers' Compensation Act nor the Americans with Disabilities Act requires that an employer create a light-duty job for someone even if that person was injured at work. However, if the employer has provided these light-duty jobs to other employees who have doctor's limitations, the employer must do the same for those people on workers' comp. If the employer refuses, you can sue the employer for retaliatory discharge. Remember that the Workers' Compensation Act provides for disability pay, retraining for another job, medical expenses, and other damages for those hurt on the job. You probably should speak with an experienced workers' comp attorney, though, to make sure your rights are fully protected.

My boss is threatening to terminate me for excessive absenteeism even though I have a workers' comp injury. Can he do this?

In most states, if you are an at will employee not covered by a union or employment contract, then your employer can terminate you for anything except discrimination. However, depending on the circumstances of your case and the existing laws, your workers' compensation case may offer you some protection. You probably should contact a local employment attorney to see if you have grounds for a suit for retaliation, for a violation of the Americans with Disabilities Act, for a violation of FMLA, or on any discrimination basis. If your workers' comp attorney has filed a complaint with the state workers' compensation commission, your case will proceed even if you have been terminated.

Chapter 14

FAMILY MEDICAL LEAVE ACT

- What is the FMLA?
- What happens to my sick days, vacation days, and short-term disability days?
- Are all employers required to allow FMLA time off?
- How can I find out more about the FMLA, and how I can use it?

What is the FMLA?

The Family Medical Leave Act (FMLA) is a federal law that allows an eligible employee a certain amount of leave—usually unpaid—for certain reasons.

Specifically, an employee who has been employed for over one year (1250 hours) can take up to twelve work weeks of unpaid leave in a twelve-month period for birth of a child, adoption, care for an immediate family member who is seriously ill, or when the employee is unable to work due to a serious health condition.

What happens to my sick days, vacation days, and short-term disability days?

Courts have held that an employer can require that an employee take paid sick time and paid vacation time along with paid disability time first, before getting unpaid leave. Recently, some courts have allowed employers to run the twelve-week FMLA time concurrent with this paid leave. This means that if an employee has one week of sick days and two weeks of paid vacation saved, not only would he or she be required to take that time off first, but it would reduce their twelve-week allotment of FMLA time by those three weeks.

Are all employers required to allow FMLA time off?

No. The employer must have a minimum of fifty employees before it is required to offer FMLA time off.

How can I find out more about the FMLA, and how I can use it?

The FMLA is enforced by the Department of Labor. On the DOL website—**www.dol.gov**—there are several pages of explanation of this act.

Section V:
Agreements between the Employer and the Employee

There may come a time when an employer and employee enter into a legal contact. This section explores the common agreements. Chapter 15 discusses noncompete agreements, which are considered protection for the business from employees who might take trade secrets, customers, and other information to the employer's competition. Chapter 16 reviews settlement agreements and severance agreements, what is meant by the standard clauses in each, and how to deal with these contracts. Finally, Chapter 17 is about mediation, arbitration, and negotiation that can result in settlement or severance agreements with the employer.

Chapter 15

NONCOMPETE AGREEMENTS

- What are noncompete agreements?
- How do I know if I am under a noncompete agreement?
- Does the noncompete agreement affect the employee after he or she quits?
- How long do noncompete agreements last?
- What other restrictions do noncompete agreements include?
- Isn't a noncompete agreement against my rights to make a living?
- Can noncompete agreements really stop an employee from taking a job with a competitor?
- What effect does an employee's noncompete agreement have on a competitor that just hired that employee?
- What can a former employer do to me if I start my own company that competes with that former employer?
- I signed a noncompete agreement that says that any litigation has to take place in the state where the employer's home office is. However, I am employed at a branch office, several states away. Is this legal?
- What does it mean to the employee if the noncompete agreement states that the laws of another state be used?
- Is there a way to avoid abiding by the noncompete agreement once I sign it?
- What is the difference between a noncompete agreement and a nonsolicitation agreement?
- Can medical professionals—like doctors and nurses—be forced to obey noncompete agreements? What happens when a hospital is included in a prohibited area?

What are noncompete agreements?

A noncompete agreement—also called a restrictive covenant—is a contract between an employee and employer that restricts the employee's association and work with competitors of the employer or in a capacity that competes with the employer when the employee decides to leave his or her job in the future.

How do I know if I am under a noncompete agreement?

Usually at the time of being hired, the employee is required to sign a document that restricts him or her from working for a competitor or from opening up his or her own competing businesses within a certain amount of time after leaving the current company. Many firms also provide a new version of this document to employees once every year or two. Also if you are terminated, laid off, downsized, or offered a severance agreement, a copy of the noncompete agreement may be provided to you.

Does the noncompete agreement affect the employee after he or she quits?

Yes. Most noncompete agreements restrict whom the employee can work for after working for the current employer by geographic location, type of industry, and time. Some of these agreements specifically mention competitors by name. The employee might also be restricted from opening up a business that directly competes with the former employer.

How long do noncompete agreements last?

Courts have found that agreements lasting between one and four years are legal. However, an employer can write a noncompete agreement for any time duration. In order to determine if that particular agreement is legal, the employee and employer would need to get a ruling from a judge.

What other restrictions do noncompete agreements include?

Many noncompete agreements restrict the employee from working in certain geographic locations. For example, if a salesperson for dairy products had Illinois, Wisconsin, and Indiana as his or her territory, the terms of his or her noncompete agreement could include that the employee not take a job for a competitor or start a dairy products company in those three states.

Isn't a noncompete agreement against my rights to make a living?

A noncompete agreement can be against your right to make a living. Several states—notably Texas and California—have found many of these agreements to be invalid because they severely restrict the former employee from making a living in his or her industry. However, this decision usually must be made by a judge. The employer must be able to protect his or her company from employees who purposely provide confidential information to a competitor as a way to get even. The law balances the employee's need to make a living with the employer's need to protect the company.

Can noncompete agreements really stop an employee from taking a job with a competitor?

This is exactly what most noncompete agreements restrict. An employee may also be restricted from sharing information about an employer with a competitor. Many noncompete agreements not only restrict an employee from working for a competitor, but they can also restrict the employee from working in a particular industry.

What effect does an employee's noncompete agreement have on a competitor that just hired that employee?

An employer that is legally enforcing a noncompete agreement can file a complaint and get a court injunction against the competitor if it can be proven that the competitor knew or should have known about the noncompete agreement but hired the employee anyway. If the competitor knew about the agreement, a judge can award the former employer damages and attorney fees to be paid by the competitor. The competitor that hires employees away from the competition as a way to move ahead in a particular industry must make sure the employees are not covered by a noncompete agreement.

What can a former employer do to me if I start my own company that competes with that former employer?

Employers that rely on noncompete agreements are very attuned to what their previous employees do. While you make think that you are successfully hiding your new company by putting it in your spouse's name or locating it at your grandmother's farm, sooner or later the former employer will find out. Your suppliers and the customers of your former employer will report you.

Your former employer will enforce the noncompete agreement by getting a temporary restraining order against you and suing you for violation of the agreement. Depending on the efficiency of the employer's attorneys, you may be facing months of delays while your new company is not allowed to do business. All your former employer needs to prove is that the noncompete agreement is reasonable and necessary to protect a legitimate business interest. Depending on the court's decision, you could end up not only losing your business, but you may also be required to pay your former employer's legal fees.

I signed a noncompete agreement that says that any litigation has to take place in the state where the employer's home office is. However, I am employed at a branch office, several states away. Is this legal?

Yes. Courts have found that an agreement between an employer and employee that includes a choice of law is legal. While the courts do review each party's connection to that state, courts will rarely change the terms of an agreement between parties. In your case the employer selected the law of the state where the home office—and probably the corporate legal department—reside. When you signed the noncompete document, you agreed to be bound by its terms, including choice of venue for any future legal actions.

What does it mean to the employee if the noncompete agreement states that the laws of another state be used?

If the noncompete agreement says that the laws of another state will be used, then if the former employer files a legal complaint against the employee, the courts in the other, named state will be used. Practically, it means that if your former employer goes to court accusing you of violating the noncompete agreement, all the litigation will be held in the other state, which means that the employee will need to get an employment attorney who is licensed in that state and be prepared to travel to that state for court appearances.

Is there a way to avoid abiding by the noncompete agreement once I sign it?

The best way to avoid abiding by an executed noncompete agreement is to have your attorney look at the agreement, map out its requirements, and look for irregularities. Many times these types of agreements are written by those who want to impress the reader with their knowledge of legalese, complex sentence structures, and numerous penalties. Courts have found that noncompete agreements that never end are not enforceable. Agreements that prohibit someone from working in any of the fifty states have also been found to be not enforceable.

If the agreement is otherwise without errors, though, you may have to follow it for the limited amount of time that it requires.

What is the difference between a noncompete agreement and a nonsolicitation agreement?

In a nonsolicitation agreement the employee may be allowed to work for a competitor or open a competing firm, but he or she is restricted from soliciting the former employer's customers for business. The only customers that are protected by this are those that the former employer can show were almost permanent customers of the company. Nonsolicitation agreements can also limit the geographic area where the former employee may look for customers.

Can medical professionals—like doctors and nurses—be forced to obey noncompete agreements? What happens when a hospital is included in a prohibited area?

Doctors and other medical professionals can be required to follow noncompete agreements. Doctors are usually required to sign noncompete agreements when they go into private practice in a group or corporation, which limits their work upon leaving the group by time and geographic location. Courts have held that when the doctor leaves a private practice, a noncompete agreement only extends to other private practice groups and not to hospitals in the area.

Chapter 16

SEVERANCE AND SETTLEMENT AGREEMENTS

- What is a severance agreement?
- What is a settlement agreement in employment law?
- Why am I being offered a severance agreement?
- What things are included in a settlement or severance agreement?
- What should I do when I get a settlement or severance agreement?
- Am I entitled to severance pay? How much severance money should I get?
- Can I get the employer to extend my health benefits as part of a severance or settlement agreement?
- Are employers required to offer severance agreements when laying off or downsizing long-term employees?
- Why does the settlement or severance agreement state that I cannot tell anyone about the terms of the agreement?
- What rights am I giving up by signing a severance agreement?
- Are there reasons to not sign a settlement or severance agreement?
- Are severance or settlement payments given over a period of time or as a lump sum?
- What are the tax and other implications of how settlement or severance payments are given?
- Am I still legally employed if my severance or settlement payments come as payroll checks for several months?
- Can I get unemployment benefits if I get a settlement or a severance package when I'm let go?

What is a severance agreement?

A severance agreement is a legal contract drawn up by an employer. The agreement offers the employee certain benefits for the employee leaving the company. The benefits are usually a set amount of money. In order to get the benefits offered, the employee must sign a legal document agreeing not to sue or file a legal complaint against the employer, plus other restrictions.

What is a settlement agreement in employment law?

A settlement agreement is a legal contract that can be drawn up by the employer's attorney or the employee's attorney. A settlement agreement offers an employee a certain benefit for the employee dropping a legal complaint against the employer. In the case of a settlement agreement, the employee will probably have an attorney conduct the negotiations with the employer. As with a severance agreement, the employee gets the benefits—usually money—after signing a legal document that may have other restrictions besides dropping the current lawsuit.

Why am I being offered a severance agreement?

Many employers that need to cut the workforce will make a determination to offer certain employees severance in exchange for leaving without filing a lawsuit. Responding to a discrimination lawsuit—even the most minor one that has no merit—can cost an employer several thousand dollars in attorney's fees and time spent to respond to the suit. Employees who are minorities, those over the age of 40, and those with disabilities are often the ones the employer is most concerned about because they have an undeniable reason to charge the employer with discrimination.

Avoiding the expense of litigation is not the only reason that employers will offer severance, though. Many employers offer severance to employees who have worked at the company for a long time, those who were considered valuable employees, and those who need a financial bridge before retirement.

Being offered a severance agreement is a great benefit and should be viewed positively, rather than wondering why one employee got it instead of another. Employers have no legal obligation to inform an employee why he or she was selected to receive a severance offer.

What things are included in a settlement or severance agreement?

Settlement and severance agreements are legal contracts and must adhere to certain contract laws. Each agreement will offer the employee certain benefits—like money—if the employee agrees to do something. In a settlement agreement, the employee must agree to drop each lawsuit or complaint and not file additional legal complaints against the employer. For a severance agreement, the employee agrees not to file any legal complaints against the employer.

In both of these situations, if the employee has already filed a workers' compensation suit, that suit must be identified in the document and allowed to proceed. In most states, once a workers' compensation suit is filed it requires a specific settlement document to remove it. This is one of those serious issues that your attorney needs to help you with.

If your employer wishes to get rid of a workers' compensation suit or a discrimination suit, and stop future lawsuits, the document must adhere to the regulations of both the workers' compensation agency and the agency or court where the discrimination suit is filed.

Other items that may be included in a settlement or severance agreement—in addition to dropping any current lawsuits and agreeing not to sue the employer—are as follows:

- a statement as to whether the employer will fight the employee's application for unemployment benefits;

- how the severance or settlement amount will be paid;

- how taxes will be withheld from the payment amount;

- that paying the money does not mean the employer admits guilt, to any violations of the law, or any future liability;

- a list of all laws—federal and state—that the employee agrees not to sue the employer under;

- that the employee agrees not to discuss the terms of the agreement with anyone other than his or her spouse, accountant, or attorney;

- other benefits—besides the money that the employee is receiving—such as health insurance, COBRA, pensions, 401(k)s and other investment plans, commissions, etc.;

- that the employee must return all company property, including cars, computers, and identification cards;

- a statement of any rehire rights;

- that if the employee violates the terms of this agreement, the case will be litigated in a particular court, usually in the state of the home office of the employer;

- that this single document covers the entire agreement between the employer and the employee, and that the employee should

not rely on any verbal promises or documents that are not referenced within the agreement; and,

- finally, if your attorney negotiated this agreement on your
behalf, there may be other items listed that are particular to
your case.

What should I do when I get a settlement or severance agreement?

In most cases a settlement agreement is something that your
attorney and the employer's attorney have worked on. Therefore,
you have someone with legal expertise assisting you and explaining
the document to you.

A severance agreement, on the other hand, may be something that
just comes out of the blue. You employer hands you these documents, provides minimal explanation, suggests you get an attorney,
and tells you that you have thirty days or less to take it or leave it.
Your next step should be to get an employment attorney to review
the document and explain what you are getting and what you are
giving up. While many severance agreements are written with care,
some employers, either on purpose or by accident, include things in a
severance agreement that the employee should be aware of.

Am I entitled to severance pay? How much severance money should I get?

The law—both federal and state—does not mandate that employees
be offered any severance pay. So, unless you and your employer
have a signed employment or union contract that requires severance
pay, you are not legally entitled to it.

That being said, in some parts of the country there are certain
calculations for severance pay that are commonly used. For example,

in some Midwest industrial areas, the most common severance pay is two weeks of pay for every complete year the employee worked for the company.

Can I get the employer to extend my health benefits as part of a severance or settlement agreement?

The most commonly offered health care benefits are offered under the Consolidated Omnibus Budget Reconciliation Act (COBRA). COBRA is not offered by every employer or in every circumstance of an employee separating from the employer. If the employee elects to take COBRA coverage, the employee must pay the usually expensive premium. The length of COBRA coverage also depends on the circumstances of the separation. For more information on COBRA go to the website **www.dol.gov/ebsa/faqs/faq_consumer_cobra.html**.

When you receive health benefits through COBRA, you are usually expected to pay the premium, instead of your employer covering all or part of it as was done when you were still employed at the company. However, a severance agreement can be drawn up to include almost anything an employee and employer can agree on, including having the employee remain on payroll until the severance is paid out, which allows the employee to continue health benefits at the current premium cost.

Sometimes the employee's attorney may be able to negotiate a better settlement deal than was first offered. However, you must be careful about looking greedy. Remember, the employer has no obligation to provide the employee with either a severance or a settlement agreement. There is a point in every negotiation when the employer thinks that it is giving up too much and may withdraw any previous offer.

Are employers required to offer severance agreements when laying off or downsizing long-term employees?

For employees who are not covered by a union or employment contract, there is no law that requires a severance package to be offered to any employee. As downsizing is becoming more common and employers are going out of business, the amount of funds available for severance agreements is drying up.

Also, the court system has not always been on the employee's side, especially when the employee is going up against a large employer. In today's economy, many employers are taking the chance that they will be able to successfully fight a discrimination lawsuit if they terminate employees. Especially in cases where the employer is cutting back on jobs across the entire company, it is easy to convince the EEOC or a state's human rights office that these terminations were done only for business reasons and not with any discriminatory intent. There are several national employers that do not bother to offer a severance package to employees they terminate until they see if the former employee is going to hire an attorney to file an EEOC complaint.

Why does the settlement or severance agreement state that I cannot tell anyone about the terms of the agreement?

In the case of a settlement agreement, the employer does not want other current employees to know that it is willing to settle a lawsuit or complaint for a certain dollar amount. Your case may be more valid than others, or your attorney might have a reputation for going after employers, so the employer may feel it is in its best interest to settle your case.

As for severance agreements, employers do not always offer everyone an agreement or the same amount of money. The employer may base the dollar amount offered as severance on the years a person was with the company, the salary level of the employee, if the employee was ever involved in any disciplinary actions, if the employee had good performance ratings, or any number of subjective factors. Since severance agreements are not required by law, they can be based on something as simple as whether or not the boss liked you.

It does no good to tell other employees when you receive a windfall severance or settlement amount. Since it is usually in the agreement that you cannot talk about it, you are taking the chance of losing the entire amount you were paid for one moment of bragging. If the other employees find out that you received a higher amount then they did, you may find yourself in the middle of their discrimination suits. When asked by co-workers about what you received, the best answer is to tell them that your attorney told you that you cannot talk about it.

What rights am I giving up by signing a severance agreement?

If you sign a severance agreement, you will be signing away every right you have to sue your employer. In the severance agreement each and every law—even laws that do not apply to you—will be listed, and by signing you will be agreeing not to sue the employer under any of those laws. In most severance agreements, the list of laws is intimidating and some employees regrettably decide they want to reserve the right to sue the employer even if that means not getting any severance.

Please remember that each severance agreement is different and is written in legal language that may intimidate even the most experienced businessperson. Before you decide whether to sign a severance agreement or not, it is recommended that you have an experienced employment attorney review the agreement and explain to you what you are giving up. Do not assume that by not signing this document, you have selected the winning trial strategy for a discrimination case. It does not always work that way.

For example, an employee may decide not to sign a severance agreement in order to file a discrimination suit based on race against the employer. Only after the employee gives up the offered severance package does he or she find out that, because employees of all races were equally terminated during a downsizing, his or her lawsuit is worthless.

Are there reasons to not sign a settlement or severance agreement?

If the amount of money offered is fair, then there are very few reasons not to sign a settlement or severance agreement. In the very rare case where you and your attorney, or you and the EEOC, are sure that you will win a discrimination or other lawsuit, you may decide not to sign the agreement. However, be warned that in litigation there are no sure things—a case that seems to be a real winner can quickly become a lost cause if the employer's legal team brings in certain evidence. Also, the jury may perceive the employee to be less than honest or just greedy for refusing a fair settlement.

Are severance or settlement payments given over a period of time or as a lump sum?

It is not uncommon for an employee to be offered a severance package that provides payments that come out of the regular payroll program. In that case, the employee continues to receive a paycheck at the normal interval along with other benefits, such as health care insurance and help finding another job. However, some employers will offer a lump-sum severance payment in order to make a clean break with the employee.

Settlement payments are normally given in a lump sum. If you and your attorney agreed that the attorney would be paid on a contingency, you will be required to share that settlement payment with your attorney. That is accomplished by either having separate checks for the attorney and the employee, or having one check where each person must cosign the check.

What are the tax and other implications of how settlement or severance payments are given?

Both settlement and severance payment amounts are considered taxable income and must be declared in your annual IRS filing. Many employers will take the normal employee taxes out of settlements and severance amounts as part of their accounting, but you should check to make sure that taxes are being withheld. Otherwise, you will be responsible for paying them at the end of the year.

Am I still legally employed if my severance or settlement payments come as payroll checks for several months?

The answer to this question depends on how your employer is listing you. Many employers will consider you an inactive employee, in which case you are still considered to be employed. If you are receiving your payments through payroll, you need to ask the following questions:

- Am I still considered an employee?

- If someone calls for me from outside the company, what will that person be told?

- What happens if I find a job while receiving this money?

- Is the employer providing me with resume or job search assistance during this time?

- Can I have use of an office during this time?

Can I get unemployment benefits if I get a settlement or a severance package when I'm let go?

Yes. Receiving a severance or settlement package does not prevent you from getting any unemployment benefits that you are already entitled to. Remember, though, that your employer can fight against you receiving unemployment benefits, and many times it will be written in your severance or settlement agreement that you agree not to apply for these benefits. You are, of course, also bound by the laws of the unemployment office in your state.

Chapter 17

MEDIATIONS, ARBITRATIONS, AND NEGOTIATIONS

- How is mediation used in employment cases?
- What can I expect in mediation?
- Is mediation used in federal government employment law cases?
- Is there any benefit to entering into mediation in an employment law case?
- When is arbitration required in an employment case?
- My employer is invoking a clause in my employment contract that requires arbitration. Is that legal?
- My union wants me to sit down for mediation before I file a discrimination suit. Is there any downside to doing that?
- Can a union representative represent me at mediation or arbitration instead of an attorney?
- What information should I provide my attorney so that he or she can enter into negotiations for me?
- Can I negotiate with my employer without my attorney?

How is mediation used in employment cases?

If you file a discrimination case with the EEOC or with your state's human rights agency, your case may qualify for its mediation program. That mediation program only selects cases where the claims are clear, both parties agree to mediate, and the agency feels mediation can work. When you agree to enter mediation, your case goes into suspension status at most agencies. This means that the days are no longer being counted toward the agency's deadline for completing the investigation.

The purpose of the mediation is for each side to present its case and work toward a compromise that will satisfy both parties. If no resolution is agreed upon at the mediation, the case will return to its open status and will be put back into the database to be assigned to an investigator. Nothing said or written at the mediation will be attached to the case file. In fact, the investigator will not even know that mediation was attempted.

What can I expect in mediation?

Formal mediations consist of a mediator, who may be a former judge, and the parties with their representatives. Witnesses usually do not attend mediation hearings.

While each mediation session is run according to how the mediator directs it, there are some general procedures that all employment mediations have in common. The person who brought the complaint (or his or her attorney) will talk about why he or she filed the suit, what happened, and why these actions broke current laws. The mediator may ask questions and bring up issues that were not mentioned. The employer (or its attorney) will tell its side of the story. Again, the mediator will probably ask the employer questions. Much of the information gathered by the mediator at this point will be facts that the parties agree upon and evidence for each side. The mediator may go back and ask each party how the events impacted their lives, what they learned from this, or what they would do differently.

In the next phase the mediator may want to discuss what each party wants. This is the compromise phase. You should go into mediation with a clear idea of what you are asking for and you are willing to compromise on. In this phase the mediator may speak with each side separately until a settlement is brokered or both sides decide to stop the mediation process.

How not to win in mediation— the worst attitudes to bring to mediation

- This is a moral issue. I am fighting for everyone who comes behind me, and I will not compromise.

- I am right, and they are wrong. There won't be any compromise. I won't even listen to their side.

- Nothing can make up for the humiliation and disrespect that I felt because of the discrimination.

- My case is so good that I will get a million dollars if I just hold out.

- Yes, I have an attorney, but I will not listen to him or her.

- Why should I participate in mediation, when it is my employer that did something wrong?

- I will lie, no one will catch me, and I will win.

Is mediation used in federal government employment law cases?

The federal government has very successful mediation programs that will get an employee a fair resolution in his or her case. For cases filed with the MSPB, the mediation program is excellent. The MSPB employs neutral mediators who are brought in from out of state. Federal employees are in the enviable position of being able to obtain top notch mediators who truly want to work toward a fair settlement.

Is there any benefit to entering into mediation in an employment law case?

This depends on the situation and the participants. Some employer's attorneys enter a mediation for a discrimination case only for the purpose of finding out what evidence the employee has against them. People who enter mediation for this purpose are not prepared to work toward a compromise, and their only purpose is to gather information.

On the other side, there are some employees who refuse to compromise. They are at the mediation only because their attorneys told them to go. These people ask for an outrageous amount of money or for things that are impossible. Worse, there are some employees who lie. They lie in the information they provide their attorneys, they sign complaints that contain lies, and they continue to lie throughout the mediation process.

Mediations that are successful are ones where both parties come into the mediation willing to try to work out a compromise that gives both sides something. There is no way to determine if mediation will work before you are in the middle of it. On a positive note, though, when mediations do work, employees can get more money in a settlement than if the settlement occurs after the employer has paid money for litigation.

When is arbitration required in an employment case?

Certain professions and some employment contracts require an arbitrator to resolve employee-employer problems. Arbitration can either be binding, which means that the parties agree to the decision of the arbitrator, or nonbinding, just like mediation.

People who work in certain professions, such as transit workers, may be required to enter binding arbitration due to a clause in their union contracts or on rare occasions when the president orders it. However, when this is the case, the arbitration involves the union representatives instead of the employee.

My employer is invoking a clause in my employment contract that requires arbitration. Is that legal?

This is a new issue for private, non-union businesses. The courts are still working out whether or not requiring arbitration is legal. Right now if your employer requires arbitration in an employment contract, you must enter arbitration before you can go into court against the employer. The problem with this, though, is timing. Many agencies require that complaints be filed within a certain time period, and arbitration may cause the employee to miss these deadlines. If you find yourself in this situation, you should contact a local employment attorney.

My union wants me to sit down for mediation before I file a discrimination suit. Is there any downside to doing that?

The only downside to waiting to file your discrimination suit is the issue of timing. If the mediation does not happen until three hundred days after the discrimination event, you will be barred from filing an EEOC complaint. At that point, you will not have any leverage over your employer. You will not be able to threaten it with a lawsuit because you will be beyond the required time limits for filing the legal complaint. While unions may discourage it, you may want to file the EEOC or other complaint before the time period expires so that you can protect your rights. Then, once you're in mediation, you can offer to drop the charges once you reach an agreement.

Can a union representative represent me at mediation or arbitration instead of an attorney?

If you are in a union, the union is supposed to represent you and may even have its own attorney who will represent you. If you feel that you are not getting adequate representation from your union, though, or if you had a private attorney file your EEOC complaint for you, you may want to bring that attorney with you to any mediation or arbitration that you are required to attend. Union representatives and union attorneys usually do not like this, but it is up to you to protect your rights.

What information should I provide my attorney so that he or she can enter into negotiations for me?

First, it is important to be totally honest with your attorney. Nothing can derail a negotiation faster than the employer producing some evidence that you did not warn your attorney about. Second, you must be willing to compromise. Look at what you want from the standpoint of reimbursement. In terms of dollar amounts, I usually ask my clients what the bare minimum is that they will accept to settle the case, and then add a cushion for negotiation purposes. The dollar amount you are asking for should be in line with your losses. Finally, you either want to give your attorney authority to settle your case for a certain amount or be in a place where your attorney can contact you for permission.

Sometimes employees who accept settlements can start to have second thoughts. They wonder if they could have gotten more money if they had just held out a little bit longer. Some change their mind after verbally accepting the offer, and later go on to reject it. This does three things:

1. it makes both the attorney and the employee look irresponsible;

2. it causes some attorneys to stop representing the employee and bill the employee for additional service; and,

3. it sends a message to the employer that the employee does not really know what he or she wants, and the employer usually will send written notice that the offer is being withdrawn.

When this happens, in most cases the employer not only does not offer any more money, but once in litigation, the employer shows the court that a fair offer was accepted and then rejected. Courts often look at this behavior as being irresponsible and greedy.

Can I negotiate with my employer without my attorney?

Of course you can. However, if you do not have training in negotiation, you may find yourself in over your head. You wouldn't do your own dentistry, so why try to be your own lawyer?

Section VI:
Looking Forward

This final section talks about the future for individual employees and the area of employment law. In Chapter 18 we try to prepare the employee for possible termination. This chapter discusses things to do to perhaps avoid a termination or at least be able to leave your job in a professional manner. We also provide information on how to begin to gather necessary evidence for potential future complaints and litigation. Chapter 19 completes this book with a look at employment law trends that should be noted by employees going forward in their careers.

Chapter 18

REMAINING EMPLOYED AND PREPARING FOR A LEGAL FIGHT

- I was just given a disciplinary warning. I want to keep my job. What should I do?
- My last performance review wasn't very good. While I did get credit for some things, most of the review made me seem lazy and ineffective. There were even some things that I consider possible lies or at least unfair comments. I am working for a new manager who would like to hire his own people. What can I do to keep my job?
- I was given a terrible performance review. I refused to sign the document. Was that the right thing to do?
- I feel that my supervisor is targeting me to be the next one terminated. What should I do?
- I consider myself a whistle-blower because I am constantly reporting violations of company rules by my supervisor to human resources. Do I have any legal protection?
- Is it always worth it to fight with your employer about how it is treating you?

I was just given a disciplinary warning. I want to keep my job. What should I do?

The first thing you need to do is be honest with yourself. Did you make a mistake? Did you do something that was against the rules? Has your performance slipped? Do you and your supervisor have a personality conflict? It is important that you honestly assess what your actions were that caused you to be disciplined or warned, because you cannot correct problems that you do not acknowledge.

If you really want to keep your job—and in this economy, keeping your job should be your top priority—you will need to take certain steps to get back in your employer's good graces. Immediately stop fighting with your employer. Even if you believe you have been accused of something unfairly, remember that as an at will employee, you can be terminated for anything except discrimination. Not fighting with your employer does not mean that you agree with his or her version of the incident that brought on the discipline. It just means that you acknowledge that your employer has the legal power to discipline you for anything and that he or she is looking at this incident from a different point of view.

Next, find out how much time you have been given to correct your performance or behavior issue. If you have been given a *Performance Improvement Plan* (PIP), there should be a schedule of things that you need to do within a certain time frame. Make sure that you keep to this time frame, and perform all the tasks required.

For those discipline actions that mention an incident and tell you not to do it again or you will be immediately terminated, the time frame to improve is immediately. Legally, if you repeat this action, not only will your employer be able to terminate you, but it probably can prevent you from getting unemployment benefits, as well.

If your employer has given you specific tasks to do to improve your performance, make sure you do them. While the tasks might be difficult and may cause you to put in extra hours, that is the way your employer has chosen for you to show improvement. If you do not know what is expected of you, find out. Go to your manager, and tell him or her that you want to work to improve whatever he or she found wrong.

Finally, pay attention to your attitude. Right now the economy is poor and companies are closing. This is not the time to stand up to an unfair employer over a disciplinary incident. The employer holds the power. Of course, if you can prove discrimination, you can always file a discrimination complaint, but filing that complaint does not help you keep your job.

My last performance review wasn't very good. While I did get credit for some things, most of the review made me seem lazy and ineffective. There were even some things that I consider possible lies or at least unfair comments. I am working for a new manager who would like to hire his own people. What can I do to keep my job?

There are a few things you can do. The first step is to stop feeling picked on and start proving that you are a good employee. Next, forget about the issue that you are being picked on because your boss wants to hire his own people. While that may be true, you diminish any response by including personal issues that you cannot prove.

Next, draft a response to your performance review. You should structure your response in the same order as the review was written. You should rebut each item that you feel was erroneous, with evidence that shows you did your job. You must provide explicit answers to each item of criticism. Your answers may include dates when various tasks were completed, any reasons that were outside of your control for missing target dates, and any supporting documents that make your case.

Do not use emotionally charged language such as, "He lied because he hates me." As much as possible state facts and supply evidence in a professional, respectful manner without emotion. As part of your rebuttal you should state that you love your job and want to continue in it. You need to also say that if there are things you need improvement on, you are willing to work to improve.

Finally, you do not want to make threats, accusations that you cannot prove, or negative comments about the person who wrote the performance review. It is better to say, "My boss may be mistaken," than to say, "That ignorant donkey couldn't find a deadline if it came up and introduced itself." Do not threaten litigation in writing or threaten to quit. You should acknowledge that you and the boss may at times disagree, but that does not mean that either person is wrong, but merely looking at things differently. You want to assure your employer that you will do all in your power to change what your boss thinks about your work. Be cooperative not combative.

Provide a copy of the rebuttal to the person who wrote your performance review and to the human resources department. Ask that a copy be placed into your permanent file with the performance review. That way when this boss leaves, your new manager can read your side.

I was given a terrible performance review. I refused to sign the document. Was that the right thing to do?

By law your signature on a performance review or on a disciplinary document only indicates that you were given the document. It does not mean that you agree with the contents. By not signing, you indicate your displeasure with the contents of the document but nothing else. In many organizations, people who refuse to sign their performance reviews are considered to be troublemakers, uncooperative, and not team players. Even if you hate every word of your review, it is better to sign the document and acknowledge that you did receive the review, and then determine how to express your opinion on the contents of the review.

Most employers have procedures in place for employees to fight or at least express their opinions about their performance reviews. These procedures can be anything from setting up a meeting with someone in human resources and having the employee fill out a form indicating what parts of the review are in question, to having the manager of the supervisor who wrote the performance review look into why the supervisor and the employee are not on the same page. Employees should follow these company procedures in addition to writing a rebuttal of the review.

Usually an employer will not alter a written performance review, no matter what evidence the employee brings in to show that the review was in error. It is possible that an employer may adjust a monetary raise that goes with the review. However, the usual response to an employee's complaint about a performance review is merely a nod of the head.

Because of this, if you are confronted with a bad review, you must do two things.

1. Determine if the reason behind the poor review is discriminatory, using the EEOC discrimination bases mentioned in Chapter 8. If you feel that the poor review is based on discrimination, you should communicate that to the human resources department and the manager of the supervisor who wrote the review.

2. Write a rebuttal to the review that includes the reasons why you feel the performance review is in error. If you feel that there is discrimination at the root of the poor review, you should include this in the rebuttal.

Five hints to keep yourself employed

1. Keep your professional knowledge and skills up to date.

2. Make sure you are aware of new technology or scientific changes in your profession.

3. Make it a habit to let your boss know about your achievements and the achievements of your subordinates and/or team.

4. Do not listen to or repeat workplace gossip.

5. Keep your resume updated at all times, especially when things are good.

I feel that my supervisor is targeting me to be the next one terminated. What should I do?

If you are an at will employee, targeting you to be the next one terminated is perfectly legal as long as the reason for the targeting is not due to discrimination. Remember that in order to file a discrimination complaint, you must be able to show a legal discrimination basis such as age, sex, race, color, religion, disability, retaliation, or another one that your state has specified.

You may want to start keeping track of what the supervisor says, the date, the time, witnesses, and what happened. If you are being discriminated against, this record may be able to help you prove your case. This is especially true when your supervisor is verbally abusing an employee and says things that are discriminatory. By consistently writing down what happens at the time of the incident, you are keeping a record that the courts will recognize, almost like an audio recording.

Finally, you may want to speak with a local employment attorney about your rights as an employee in your state. Many states have laws that give employees additional rights that we have not reviewed in this book.

I consider myself a whistle-blower because I am constantly reporting violations of company rules by my supervisor to human resources. Do I have any legal protection?

If you do have any protection, it will come from state law. Federal laws and the majority of state laws only provide whistle-blower protection to those who report their employers to authorities or government offices for violations of existing laws. These are not company policy or company rule violations, but violations of actual laws that are reported to the enforcing agency.

For example, in a trucking firm if a truck driver reports an ineffective truck repair that causes violations of the state laws to the Department of Transportation in that state, that truck driver is a whistle-blower. On the other hand, if the truck driver merely reports the problem to the vice president of truck maintenance, that does not qualify for whistle-blower protection under the law.

Be careful with reporting your supervisor to the human resources department constantly. Your employer may consider these multiple reports regarding your supervisor to be a negative mark on you instead of on your supervisor. For some employers, constantly complaining about your supervisor is an indication of a problem with your attitude or that you do not have enough work to keep you busy. While it is great to be cognizant of the company rules, unless you have been appointed as the company police, your reporting of others may show that you are not a team player.

Is it always worth it to fight with your employer about how it is treating you?

It is accurate to say that at one time or another every employee is unhappy or annoyed with what goes on at work. These problems can come from the owners, managers, supervisors, co-workers, the amount of work to be done, or any irritant. Even the building where the work is done may cause problems. The employee must evaluate the problem. Is it an issue that can be resolved by an attorney? Does an attorney even need to be involved? Is it a health issue? Is it a legal issue? Is it something that can be fixed?

I receive many calls from employees who believe that they have legitimate legal grievances against their employers only to find out that the grievance is not covered by any current laws. This could be due to the employer not having a sufficient number of employees or that the unfair action is not considered to be discrimination by the law. Many times these issues involve departments where one group of employees gossips about another group who are all the same in age, sex, race, etc. Or it can be an issue of certain employees being friends with some people and not with others. These may be issues that not only are not covered by the law but are not even covered by the company rules.

For most employees, once they find out that their complaints cannot go anywhere in the court system, they drop the fight and go on working at the same company. However, there are some people who continue to fight even when there is no legitimate way to resolve their issues in a legal venue. The continuation of fighting may include filing lots of internal grievances, writing memos, spending time concentrating on the problem rather than work, or merely telling anyone who will listen about the issue. Or the continuation of fighting may include meeting with several attorneys until the employee finds one who is willing to sue the employer.

From the employer's standpoint it is difficult to keep an employee who spends time being disgruntled and spreading his or her negativity to other workers. It is hard on the employer to have an employee who will not let go of a problem, especially when the problem has no real solution. This snowballs into poor reviews, promotions not given, and other lost career benefits, which in turn gives the disgruntled employee additional issues to complain about.

We are living in an economy where employers can outsource thousands of jobs, lay off entire plants, or terminate large numbers of people without any warning and without any employment law consequences. Employees must keep this in mind every day. There is no guarantee that work will ever be a fun place to be, and there is no guarantee that your boss will be fair. Once you have looked at all your options and have been told that there is nothing that can be done about the problem, you need to let it go and get back to work. I will leave you with what an Illinois appellate judge once told me: "In employment law, unfair is not always illegal."

Chapter 19

THE FUTURE OF EMPLOYMENT LAW

Employment law—like every other field of law—is evolving every day. The federal and state legislators pass new laws or amendments on existing laws. The agencies that have been tasked to enforce these laws issue directives that explain how the laws should be interpreted. The federal and state courts also interpret these same laws. Those of us who work in this field spend a good portion of each week simply reading what is going on in our profession.

Much of what will come in the future for employment law is being influenced by our economy, the stability of the world, the stock markets, and who is in charge in Washington. That being said, here is what I predict we can expect in the next few years.

- The cost of health care will continue to be an issue. The legislators and the courts will be slow to see any downside to employers promoting healthful behaviors through rewards and punishments.

- Some states will provide additional paid and unpaid leave, similar to the FMLA. Some of this paid leave may be sponsored by the state and paid for by employees.

- The courts will finally address the issue of employers that run an employee's allotted FMLA time off concurrently with vacation or sick time for an employee who is out of work due to a medical condition.

- In the distant future, the issue of penalizing the overweight or the smokers with financial costs may become an issue of discrimination. However, this is far on the horizon.

- The next addition to the discrimination bases for the EEOC will be sexual orientation, followed by an additional penalty for military discrimination. A large number of states already have these two discrimination bases added to their laws.

- Existing laws will be modified to provide additional protection for returning military, families of service members, and disabled service members. In January 2008, President Bush signed an extension to the Family and Medical Leave Act to allow additional leave for family members caring for members of the military who were injured on duty and under other circumstances.

- There will be a tightening on what an employer can use in conducting a background check of potential employees.

- The EEOC will continue to look for creative ways to reduce its backlog of discrimination cases. While some offices have already tried stronger initial reviews and allowing investigators in other locations to assist, there is no universal consensus on how to resolve the exponentially growing number of complaints that the EEOC receives.

- States who are finding it hard to process all the discrimination complaints will provide options to employees who wish to pursue their claims in a local court. Several states have already given employees the option to file their complaints in a state civil court instead of waiting for the state agency to perform the investigation. This will increase the cost to those employees who take this option, but will clear some of the backlog.

- The next hot topic in Washington will be how to keep U.S. businesses from outsourcing large numbers of jobs to foreign countries while causing massive layoffs here. Some suggestions considered will include penalties, taxes, and the limitation of stock trading.

Glossary

A

accrued vacation days. The vacation days that an employee has earned and that are owed to the employee. The requirements to earn these days are set by the employer following the Department of Labor rules.

Age Discrimination in Employment Act of 1967 (ADEA). Act that protects individuals who are 40 years of age or older.

Americans with Disabilities Act (ADA) of 1990 (Title I and Title V). Act that prohibits employment discrimination against qualified individuals with disabilities in the private sector and in state and local governments.

appeal. A legal function by which the court is asked to review a past decision.

application. The form that a potential employee must fill out in order to apply for a job.

at will. A term that indicates that the employee is not a union member, is covered under a union contract, or is not covered under an employment contract. The majority of states have at will employment because the state laws that protect the employees who work in the state do not provide any additional protection to the employees than what is provided by federal law.

B

background check. A detailed report provided by a professional regarding a potential employee. Information contained on the report can include former jobs, current address, current employer, and any criminal charges.

bankruptcy. A legal procedure for reorganizing and lowering debt under court supervision.

basis of discrimination. Under federal law, an employer cannot discriminate against employees based on age, color, disability, equal pay, national origin, pregnancy, sex, race, religion, or retaliation.

breach of contract. A legal complaint filed in a lawsuit against a person who does not follow the terms of a contract.

C

cause. Used in the phrase "fired for cause." It is a legitimate reason for terminating an employee. Cause can be a violation of the company rules or policies, or—for an at will employee—due to any other reason.

Civil Rights Act of 1991. Act that provides monetary damages in cases of intentional employment discrimination.

contingency. An agreement where the attorney takes a case for a minor amount or no up-front money, but receives a sizable portion of any settlement.

D

defendant. The person being sued or who is the subject of a complaint.

Department of Labor (DOL). A federal government agency.

discrimination complaint. A legal document that an employee files with federal or state agencies and that accuses his or her employer of violating discrimination laws.

downsizing. The termination of an employee due to a business issue that involved a restructuring or reassignment of jobs within the company.

drug testing. A test used by an employer to determine if a person can be hired. It can also be used after the person is hired as a way to deter employees from doing drugs and as a safety issue to prevent on-the-job accidents.

dual filing. A legal strategy used by attorneys to file the same complaint in multiple places. For example, a discrimination complaint may be filed with both the state agency in the state where the employee lives and with the federal EEOC.

E

employment contract. A written agreement between an employer and an employee regarding the detailed terms of employment.

employee handbook. A book that details the rules and policies of the employer.

employment attorney. An attorney who concentrates on employment law cases.

Equal Employment Opportunity Commission (EEOC). The federal agency that enforces all federal employment discrimination laws.

Equal Pay Act of 1963 (EPA). Act that protects men and women who perform substantially equal work in the same establishment from sex-based wage discrimination.

G

government agency. The generic title for the different groups in the government. For example, the Department of Justice and the Department of Labor are federal government agencies.

government employee. A person who works for the state or federal government directly as an employee.

grievance. A formal complaint by an employee, either through his or her union or directly to human resources.

H

hourly rate. The rate attorneys charge for their work.

human resources. The department or person in a company who handles personnel work.

I

inactive status. An employee who is still technically on the payroll but is not working. This status can be assigned to an employee when he or she is on a medical leave, on a sabbatical, or being paid a severance over a period of time. In most states, the employee who is on inactive status is still considered to be employed by the company and does not qualify for unemployment benefits.

indigent. A person who has met the financial requirements for free or inexpensive legal assistance.

L

layoff. An event where the employer terminates or eliminates the jobs of a group of people. Usually used when referring to union members, who can have *recall rights* in a layoff. A layoff can be permanent (when the jobs are eliminated) or temporary (when the layoff is due to a business problem or economic downturn).

M

mediation. Process used in legal cases to try to obtain a settlement between the parties instead of filing a lawsuit.

N

nepotism. Providing benefits to a person because he or she is related to someone. An example is the person who is hired into his father's company and is quickly promoted to a management position.

notice. A document that the employee gives to the employer, saying that the employee quits the job, or that the employer gives to the employee, saying that the employee is fired.

P

payroll system. Generic term for the method an employer uses to pay employees.

plaintiff. The person who files the lawsuit or complaint.

pro bono. Legal term that indicates the attorney is not being paid for his or her work.

probationary period. The time that a new employee is being tested by an employer. This period can range from weeks to months, depending on the employer. While in probation, an employee may not have all the benefits of a regular employee.

pro se. Legal term that indicates that a person is representing him- or herself in a legal case without an attorney.

R

recall rights. Typically part of a union contract. An employee who has recall rights will be called back to work in the event of a layoff that is deemed to be temporary.

reference. A letter written or statement made by an employer about a former employee.

Rehabilitation Act of 1973. An act that prohibits discrimination against qualified individuals with disabilities who work in the federal government.

relief. Common term used in a court case to indicate what the person who is suing wants.

relocate. To move to another physical area.

restructuring. A change in the duties or tasks required of someone in a particular position.

retainer. The amount of money provided to an attorney up front that the attorney bills against as the case progresses. When the retainer has been used up, the client must pay the attorney additional money.

retainer agreement. A written contract between an attorney and a client detailing the fees that will be charged and the work that will be provided.

right to sue letter. A document issued by the EEOC that allows a plaintiff to file a lawsuit in the federal district court. This letter usually indicates that the EEOC found nothing that it is willing to pursue in court, but that the person who filed the complaint can pay for his or her own attorney to go to the next step.

S

seniority. Indicates how long a person has been employed at a company or in a particular job. For union members, an employee's seniority is very important and can control important issues such as pay and being able to retain a job in a layoff. For at will employees, seniority means nothing under the law.

severance agreement. A legal document written by an employer that provides certain benefits to an employee when the employee is terminated from his or her job. To obtain these benefits the employee must agree to the terms in the agreement.

T

temporary agency. An employer rents out employees to other employers for various jobs and for various time frames.

temporary restraining order (TRO). A court order not used in employment law. Commonly used in family or criminal law cases when the court orders that someone do something or stop doing something immediately.

termination. Firing of the employee by the employer. This term can be viewed negatively by potential employers, if the employee was fired for cause.

termination notice. The paper document from the employer that tells an employee that he or she is fired. This document is not required under the law since terminations can be verbal.

time limits/statute of limitations. Each law and each agency has a set time in which a complaint can be filed. After this set amount of time has expired, a complaint can no longer be filed. For example, the EEOC will only allow discrimination complaints about an event that occurred within the last three hundred days. These time limits vary by agency and the type of complaint.

Title VII of the Civil Rights Act of 1964. Prohibits employment discrimination based on race, color, religion, sex, or national origin.

U

unemployment benefits. Financial benefits provided to those who are no longer employed. Each state follows its own rules about qualifying for these benefits in addition to the federal directives.

Appendix A

WHERE TO FILE DISCRIMINATION COMPLAINTS BY STATE

This appendix contains a list of the state offices where employees can file discrimination complaints. For federal Equal Employment Opportunity Commission (EEOC) offices, go to **www.eeoc.gov**.

The list is organized by state name. Even with double- and triple-checking, sometimes a website is closed prior to publication or shortly after. If the website listed does not work, you can either go to your state's official website—which is usually www.name of your state.gov—or do an Internet search on your state's name plus the words "discrimination complaint."

ALABAMA

Discrimination/Harassment—
State Agency
**Alabama Department of
Human Resources**
Office of Equal Employment
and Civil Rights
334-242-1550
www.dhr.alabama.gov/page.
asp?pageid=198

Local Offices of EEOC
Birmingham District Office
Ridge Park Place
1130 22nd Street, Suite 2000
Birmingham, AL 35202
800-669-4000

Mobile Local Office
63 South Royal Street, Suite 504
Mobile, AL 36602
800-669-4000

ALASKA

Discrimination/Harassment—
State Agency
Alaska uses EEOC offices for
discrimination complaints.
www.jobs.state.ak.us/eo

Local Office of EEOC
San Francisco District Office
350 The Embarcadero, Suite
500
San Francisco, CA 94015
415-356-5100

ARIZONA

Discrimination/Harassment—
State Agency
**Office of the Attorney General,
Civil Rights Division (CRD),
Phoenix**
1275 West Washington Street
Phoenix, AZ 85007
602-542-5263
877-491-5742

**Office of the Attorney General,
Civil Rights Division (CRD),
Tucson**
400 West Congress, Suite S215
Tucson, AZ 85701
520-628-6500
877-491-5740
www.azag.gov/civil_rights

Local Office of EEOC
Phoenix District Office
3300 North Central Avenue,
Suite 690
Phoenix, AZ 85012
602-640-5000

ARKANSAS

Discrimination/Harassment—
State Agency
Arkansas has no state agency
that enforces antidiscrimination
laws; see the local EEOC office
below.

Local Office of EEOC
**Equal Employment Opportunity
Commission (EEOC)**
Little Rock Area Office
820 Louisiana Street, Suite 200
Little Rock, AR 72201
800-669-4000

CALIFORNIA

Discrimination/Harassment—
State Agency
**Department of Fair
Employment and Housing,
Headquarters**
2218 Kausen Drive, Suite 100
Elk Grove, CA 95758
916-478-7251
www.dfeh.ca.gov

**Bakersfield DFEH District
Office**
4800 Stockdale Highway,
Suite 215
Bakersfield, CA 93309
661-395-2729
800-884-1684

Fresno DFEH District Office
1320 East Shaw Avenue,
Suite 150
Fresno, CA 93710
559-244-4760
800-884-1684

**Los Angeles DFEH District
Office**
611 West 6th Street, Suite 1500
Los Angeles, CA 90017
213-439-6799
800-884-1684

Oakland DFEH District Office
1515 Clay Street, Suite 701
Oakland, CA 94612
510-622-2941
800-884-1684

Sacramento DFEH District Office
2000 O Street, Suite 120
Sacramento, CA 95814
916-445-5523
800-884-1684

San Diego DFEH District Office
1350 Front Street, Suite 3005
San Diego, CA 92101
619-645-2681
800-884-1684

San Francisco DFEH District Office
1515 Clay Street, Suite 701
Oakland, CA 94612
510-622-2973
800-884-1684

San Jose DFEH District Office
2570 North First Street, Suite 480
San Jose, CA 95131
408-325-0344

Santa Ana DFEH District Office
2101 East 4th Street, Suite 255-B
Santa Ana, CA 92705
714-558-4266
800-884-1684

Local Offices of EEOC
Fresno Local Office
2300 Tulare Street, Suite 215
Fresno, CA 93721
800-669-4000

Los Angeles District Office
Roybal Federal Building
255 East Temple Street, 4th Floor
Los Angeles, CA 90012
213-894-1000

Oakland Local Office
1301 Clay Street, Suite 1170-N
Oakland, CA 94612
510-637-3230

San Diego Local Office
401 B Street, Suite 510
San Diego, CA 92101
619-557-7235

San Francisco District Office
350 The Embarcadero, Suite 500
San Francisco, CA 94105
415-356-5100

San Jose Local Office
96 North 3rd Street, Suite 200
San Jose, CA 95112
408-291-7352

COLORADO

Discrimination/Harassment—
State Agency
Civil Rights Division
1560 Broadway, Suite 1050
Denver, CO 80202
303-894-2997
800-262-4845
www.dora.state.co.us/civil-
rights/index.htm

Local Office of EEOC
Denver Field Office
303 East 17th Avenue,
Suite 510
Denver, CO 80203
303-866-1300

CONNECTICUT

Discrimination/Harassment—
State Agency
**Connecticut Commission
on Human Rights and
Opportunities (CHRO)**
21 Grand Street
Hartford, CT 06106
860-541-3400
800-477-5737
www.state.ct.us/chro/index.html

Local Office of EEOC
New York District Office
33 Whitehall Street, 5th Floor
New York, NY 10004
800-669-4000

DELAWARE

Discrimination/Harassment—
State Agency
Delaware Department of Labor
Office of Labor Law
Enforcement (OLLE),
Milford Office
13 Southwest Front Street,
Suite 101
Milford, DE 19963
302-422-1134

Delaware Department of Labor
Office of Labor Law
Enforcement (OLLE),
Newark Office
225 Corporate Boulevard,
Suite 104
Newark, DE 19702

www.delawareworks.com/
industrialaffairs/services/
LaborLawEnforcement.shtml

Delaware Department of Labor
Office of Labor Law
Enforcement (OLLE),
Wilmington Office
4425 North Market Street,
3rd Floor
Wilmington, DE 19802
302-761-8200

Local Offices of EEOC
Philadelphia District Office
801 Market Street, Suite 1300
Philadelphia, PA 19107
215-440-2600

FLORIDA

Discrimination/Harassment—
State Agency
**Florida Commission on Human
Relations**
2009 Apalachee Parkway,
Suite 200

Tallahassee, FL 32301
850-488-7082
800-342-8170
http://fchr.state.fl.us

Local Offices of EEOC
Miami District Office
One Biscayne Tower

2 South Biscayne Boulevard,
Suite 2700
Miami, FL 33131
305-536-4491

Tampa Field Office
501 East Polk Street, Suite
1000
Tampa, FL 33602
813-228-2310

GEORGIA

Discrimination/Harassment—
State Agency
Georgia has no state agency that
enforces antidiscrimination laws
for private sector (nongovernment) employees; see the local
EEOC offices below.

Local Offices of EEOC
Atlanta District Office
Sam Nunn Atlanta Federal
Center

100 Alabama Street, Suite 4R30
Atlanta, GA 30303
404-562-6800

Savannah Local Office
410 Mall Boulevard, Suite G
Savannah, GA 31406
912-652-4234

HAWAII

Discrimination/Harassment—
State Agency
**Hawaii Civil Rights
Commission**
830 Punchbowl Street, Room 411
Honolulu, HI 96813
808-586-8636
www.hawaii.gov/hcrc

Local Offices of EEOC
Honolulu Local Office
300 Ala Moana Boulevard,
Room 7-127
P.O. Box 50082
Honolulu, HI 96850
808-541-3120

IDAHO

Discrimination/Harassment—
State Agency
Idaho Human Rights Commission
1109 Main Street, Fourth Floor
Boise, ID 83702
208-334-2873
888-249-7025
http://www2.state.id.us/ihrc/
ihrchome.htm

Local Office of EEOC
Seattle Field Office
Federal Office Building
909 First Avenue, Suite 400
Seattle, WA 98104
206-220-6883

ILLINOIS

Discrimination/Harassment—
State Agency
**Illinois Department of Human
Rights (IDHR), Chicago Office**
James R. Thompson Center
100 West Randolph Street,
Suite 10-100
Chicago, IL 60601
312-814-6200

**Illinois Department of Human
Rights, Marion Office**
Marion State Regional
Office Building
2309 West Main Street, Suite 112
Marion, IL 62959
618-993-7463

**Illinois Department of Human
Rights, Springfield Office**
222 South College, Floor 1
Springfield, IL 62704
217-785-5100
www.state.il.us/dhr

Local Offices of EEOC
Chicago District Office
500 West Madison Street,
Suite 2000
Chicago, IL 60661
312-353-2713

St. Louis District Office
Robert A. Young Building
1222 Spruce Street, Room 8.100
St. Louis, MO 63103
314-539-7800

INDIANA

Discrimination/Harassment—
State Agency
State of Indiana Civil Rights Commission
Indiana Government Center
North
100 North Senate Avenue,
Room N103
Indianapolis, IN 46204
317-232-2600
800-628-2909
www.state.in.us/icrc

Local Office of EEOC
Indianapolis District Office
101 West Ohio Street,
Suite 1900
Indianapolis, IN 46204
317-226-7212

IOWA

Discrimination/Harassment—
State Agency
Iowa Civil Rights Commission
Grimes State Office Building
400 East 14th Street
Des Moines, IA 50319
515-281-4121
800-457-4416
www.state.ia.us/government/
crc/index.html

Local Office of EEOC
Milwaukee Area Office
Reuss Federal Plaza
310 West Wisconsin Avenue,
Suite 800
Milwaukee, WI 53203
414-297-1111

KANSAS

Discrimination/Harassment—
State Agency
**Kansas Human Rights
Commission (KHRC), Main
Office (Topeka)**
900 Southwest Jackson, Suite
568-S
Topeka, KS 66612
785-296-3206
888-793-6874

**Kansas Human Rights
Commission, Dodge City Office**
100 Military Plaza, Suite 220
Dodge City, KS 67801
620-225-4804

**Kansas Human Rights
Commission, Independence
Office**
200 Arco Place, Suite 311
Independence, KS 67301
620-331-7083

**Kansas Human Rights
Commission, Wichita Office**
130 South Market, Suite 7050
Wichita, KS 67202
316-337-6270
www.khrc.net

Local Office of EEOC
Kansas City Area Office
Gateway Tower II
4th & State Avenue, Suite 905
Kansas City, KS 66101
913-551-5655

KENTUCKY

Discrimination/Harassment—
State Agency
**Kentucky Commission on
Human Rights, Main Office
(Louisville)**
332 West Broadway, 7th Floor
Louisville, KY 40202
502-595-4024
800-292-5566
http://kchr.ky.gov/

**Kentucky Commission on Human
Rights, Northern Kentucky**
636 Madison Avenue, Suite 401
Covington, KY 41011
859-292-2935

Local Offices of EEOC
Indianapolis District Office
101 West Ohio Street, Suite 1900
Indianapolis, IN 46204
800-669-4000

Louisville Area Office
600 Dr. Martin Luther King Jr.
Place, Suite 268
Louisville, KY 40202
502-582-6082

LOUISIANA

Discrimination/Harassment—
State Agency
**Louisiana Commission on
Human Rights**
1001 North 23rd Street,
Suite 262
Baton Rouge, LA 70802
225-342-6969
www.gov.state.la.us/

HumanRights/humanright-
shome.htm

Local Office of EEOC
New Orleans Field Office
1555 Poydras Street, Suite 1900
New Orleans, LA 70112
504-589-2329

MAINE

Discrimination/Harassment—
State Agency
**Maine Human Rights
Commission**
#51 State House Station
Augusta, ME 04333
207-624-6050
www.state.me.us/mhrc/
index.shtml

Local Office of EEOC
Boston Area Office
John F. Kennedy Federal
Building
475 Government Center
Boston, MA 02203
617-565-3200

MARYLAND

Discrimination/Harassment—
State Agency
**Maryland Commission on
Human Rights, Baltimore
Office**
William Donald Schaefer
Towers
6 Saint Paul Street, Suite 900
Baltimore, MD 21202
410-767-8600
800-637-6247

**Maryland Commission on
Human Rights, Hagerstown
Office**
44 North Potomac Street,
Suite 202
Hagerstown, MD 21740
301-797-8521

**Maryland Commission on Human
Rights, Leonardtown Office**
Joseph P. Carter Center
23110 Leonard Hall Drive
P.O. Box 653
Leonardtown, MD 20650
301-880-2740

Maryland Commission on Human Rights, Salisbury Office
201 Baptist Street, Suite 33
Salisbury, MD 21801
410-713-3611
www.mchr.state.md.us

Local Office of EEOC
Baltimore Field Office
City Crescent Building
10 South Howard Street,
3rd Floor
Baltimore, MD 21201
410-962-3932

MASSACHUSETTS

Discrimination/Harassment—
State Agency
Massachusetts Commission Against Discrimination (MCAD), Boston Office
One Ashburton Place,
Room 601
Boston, MA 02108
617-994-6000

Massachusetts Commission Against Discrimination, Springfield Office
436 Dwight Street, Room 220
Springfield, MA 01103
413-739-2145

Massachusetts Commission Against Discrimination, Worcester Office
455 Main Street, Room 100
Worcester, MA 01608
508-799-8010
www.state.ma.us/mcad

Local Office of EEOC
Boston Area Office
John F. Kennedy Federal
Building
475 Government Center
Boston, MA 02203
617-565-3200

MICHIGAN

Discrimination/Harassment—
State Agency
**Michigan Department of Civil
Rights (MDCR), Benton
Harbor Office**
499 West Main Street
Benton Harbor, MI 49022
269-925-7044

**Michigan Department of Civil
Rights, Detroit Service Center**
Cadillac Place
3054 West Grand Boulevard,
Suite 3-600
Detroit, MI 48202
313-456-3700

**Michigan Department of Civil
Rights, Flint Office**
Flint State Office Building,
7th Floor
125 East Union
Flint, MI 48502
810-760-2805

**Michigan Department of Civil
Rights, Grand Rapids Office**
State Office Building, 4th Floor
350 Ottawa, Northwest
Grand Rapids, MI 49503
616-356-0380

**Michigan Department of Civil
Rights, Kalamazoo Office**
535 South Burdick Street,
Suite 230
Kalamazoo, MI 49007
269-337-3640

**Michigan Department of Civil
Rights, Lansing Office**
Capital Tower Building
110 West Michigan Avenue,
Suite 800
Lansing, MI 48933
517-241-6300

**Michigan Department of Civil
Rights, Marquette Office**
1504 West Washington Street,
Suite B
Marquette, MI 49855
906-226-6393

Michigan Department of Civil Rights, Saginaw Office
State Office Building
411 East Genesee Avenue
Saginaw, MI 48607
989-758-1686

Michigan Department of Civil Rights, Traverse City Office
State Office Building
701 South Elmwood, Suite 10, Room 410

Traverse City, MI 49685
231-922-5211
www.michigan.gov/mdcr

Local Office of EEOC
Detroit Field Office
Patrick V. McNamara Building
477 Michigan Avenue, Room 865
Detroit, MI 48226
313-226-7636

MINNESOTA

Discrimination/Harassment—
State Agency
Minnesota Department of Human Rights (MDHR)
Army Corps of Engineers Centre
190 East 5th Street, Suite 700
Saint Paul, MN 55101
651-296-5663
800-657-3704
www.humanrights.state.mn.us

Local Office of EEOC
Minneapolis Area Office
330 South Second Avenue, Suite 720
Minneapolis, MN 55401
612-335-4040

MISSISSIPPI

Discrimination/Harassment—
State Agency

Mississippi has no state agency
that enforces antidiscrimination
laws; see the local EEOC office
below.

Local Office of EEOC
Jackson Area Office
Dr. A.H. McCoy Federal
Building
100 West Capitol Street, Suite
207
Jackson, MS 39269
601-965-4537

MISSOURI

Discrimination/Harassment—
State Agency
**Missouri Commission on
Human Rights (MCHR), Main
Office (Jefferson City)**
P.O. Box 1129
3315 West Truman Boulevard
Jefferson City, MO 65102573-
751-3325

**Missouri Commission on Human
Rights, Kansas City Office**
1410 Genessee, Suite 260
Kansas City, MO 64102
816-889-5100

**Missouri Commission on
Human Rights, Sikeston Office**
106 Arthur Drive
Sikeston, MO 63801
573-472-5320

**Missouri Commission on Human
Rights, Springfield Office**
P.O. Box 1300
Ozark, MO 65721
573-751-3325

**Missouri Commission on
Human Rights, St. Louis Office**
111 North 7th Street, Suite 903
St. Louis, MO 63101
314-340-7590

877-781-4236 (toll-free discrimination complaint hotline—
messages checked weekly):
www.dolir.mo.gov/hr/index.htm

Local Offices of EEOC
Kansas City Area Office
4th & State Avenue, 9th Floor
Kansas City, KS 66101
913-551-5655

St. Louis District Office
Robert A. Young Building
1222 Spruce Street,
Room 8.100
St. Louis, MO 63103
314-539-7800

MONTANA

Discrimination/Harassment—
State Agency
**Montana Department of Labor
and Industry**
Human Rights Bureau (HRB)
1625 11th Avenue
P.O. Box 1728
Helena, MT 59624
406-444-2884
800-542-0807
http://erd.dli.mt.gov/human-
right/hrhome.asp

Local Office of EEOC
Seattle Field Office
Federal Office Building
909 First Avenue, Suite 400
Seattle, WA 98104
206-220-6883

NEBRASKA

Discrimination/Harassment—
State Agency
**Nebraska Equal Opportunity
Commission (NEOC), Main
Office (Lincoln)**
Nebraska State Office Building
301 Centennial Mall South,
5th Floor
P.O. Box 94934
Lincoln, NE 68509
402-471-2024
800-642-6112

**Nebraska Equal Opportunity
Commission, Omaha Office**
Downtown Education Center/
State Office Building
1313 Farnam Street, 3rd Floor
Omaha, NE 68102
402-595-2028
800-382-7820

**Nebraska Equal Opportunity
Commission, Scottsbluff Office**
Panhandle State Office
Complex
4500 Avenue "I"
P.O. Box 1500
Scottsbluff, NE 69363
308-632-1340
www.nol.org/home/NEOC

Local Office of EEOC
Denver Field Office
303 East 17th Avenue,
Suite 510
Denver, CO 80203
303-866-1300

NEVADA

Discrimination/Harassment—
State Agency
**Nevada Equal Rights
Commission (NERC),
Las Vegas Office**
2800 St. Louis Avenue
Las Vegas, NV 89104
702-486-7161

**Nevada Equal Rights
Commission, Reno Office**
1325 Corporate Boulevard,
Room 115
Reno, NV 89502
775-823-6690
www.detr.state.nv.us/nerc.htm

Local Offices of EEOC
Las Vegas Local Office
333 Las Vegas Boulevard South,
Suite 8112
Las Vegas, NV 89101
800-669-4000

San Francisco District Office
350 The Embarcadero, Suite 500
San Francisco, CA 94105
415-356-5100

NEW HAMPSHIRE

Discrimination/Harassment—
State Agency
**New Hampshire Commission
for Human Rights**
2 Chenell Drive
Concord, NH 03301
603-271-2767
http://webster.state.nh.us/hrc/
index.html

Local Office of EEOC
Boston Area Office
John F. Kennedy Federal
Building
475 Government Center
Boston, MA 02203
617-565-3200

NEW JERSEY

Discrimination/Harassment—
State Agency
**New Jersey Division on Civil
Rights (DCR), Atlantic City
Satellite Office**
26 Pennsylvania Avenue, 3rd
Floor
Atlantic City, NJ 08401
609-441-3100

**New Jersey Division on Civil
Rights, Camden Regional Office**
1 Port Center, 4th Floor
2 Riverside Drive, Suite 402
Camden, NJ 08103
856-614-2550

**New Jersey Division on
Civil Rights, Jersey City
Neighborhood Office**
574 Newark Avenue
Jersey City, NJ 07306

**New Jersey Division on Civil
Rights, Newark Regional Office**
31 Clinton Street
P.O. Box 46001
Newark, NJ 07102
973-648-2700

**New Jersey Division on Civil
Rights, Paterson Regional
Office**
100 Hamilton Plaza, 8th Floor
Paterson, NJ 07505
973-977-4500

**New Jersey Division on Civil
Rights, Trenton Regional Office**
140 East Front Street
P.O. Box 090
Trenton, NJ 08625
609-292-4605
www.state.nj.us/lps/dcr/index.
html

Local Office of EEOC
Newark Area Office
One Newark Center, 21st Floor
Newark, NJ 07102
973-645-6383

NEW MEXICO

Discrimination/Harassment—
State Agency
New Mexico
Department of Labor
Human Rights Division
1596 Pacheco Street
Aspen Plaza, Suite 103
Santa Fe, NM 87505
505-827-6838
800-566-9471
www.dol.state.nm.us/dol_hrd.
html

Local Office of EEOC
Albuquerque Area Office
505 Marquette Street,
Northwest, Suite 900
Albuquerque, NM 87102
505-248-5201

Dallas District Office
207 South Houston Street,
3rd Floor
Dallas TX, 75202
214-655-3355

NEW YORK

Discrimination/Harassment—
State Agency
New York Division of Human
Rights (DHR), Headquarters
(Bronx Office)
One Fordham Plaza, 4th Floor
Bronx, NY 10458
718-741-8400

New York Division of Human
Rights, Albany Regional Office
Corning Tower, 28th Floor
Empire State Plaza

P.O. Box 20409
Albany, NY 12220
518-474-2705

New York Division of Human
Rights, Buffalo Office
The Walter J. Mahoney State
Office Building
65 Court Street, Suite 506
Buffalo, NY 14202
716-847-7632

New York Division of Human Rights, Long Island Office
State Office Building
Veterans Memorial Highway,
Suite 3A-15
Hauppauge, NY 11787
631-952-6434

New York Division of Human Rights, Manhattan Office
Adam Clayton Powell State
Office Building
163 West 125th Street, 4th
Floor
New York, NY 10027
212-961-8650

New York Division of Human Rights, Peekskill Office
8 John Walsh Boulevard,
Suite 204
Peekskill, NY 10566
914-788-8050

New York Division of Human Rights, Syracuse Office
333 East Washington Street,
Room 443
Syracuse, NY 13202
315-428-4633
www.dhr.state.ny.us

Local Offices of EEOC
Buffalo Local Office
6 Fountain Plaza, Suite 350
Buffalo, NY 14202
716-551-4441

New York District Office
33 Whitehall Street, 5th Floor
New York, NY 10004
212-336-3620

NORTH CAROLINA

Discrimination/Harassment—
State Agency

North Carolina has no state
agency that enforces antidiscrimination laws; see the local
EEOC offices below.

Local Offices of EEOC
Charlotte District Office
129 West Trade Street,
Suite 400
Charlotte, NC 28202
704-344-6682

Greensboro Local Office
2303 West Meadowview Road,
Suite 201
Greensboro, NC 27407
336-547-4188

Raleigh Area Office
1309 Annapolis Drive
Raleigh, NC 27608
919-856-4064

NORTH DAKOTA

Discrimination/Harassment—
State Agency
**North Dakota Department of
Labor**
Human Rights Division
600 East Boulevard Avenue,
Department 406
Bismarck, ND 58505
701-328-2660
800-582-8032
www.state.nd.us/labor/services/
human-rights/employment-disc.
html

Local Office of EEOC
Minneapolis Area Office
Towle Building
330 South Second Avenue,
Suite 720
Minneapolis, MN 55401
612-335-4040

OHIO

Discrimination/Harassment—
State Agency
**Ohio Civil Rights Commission
(OCRC), Central Office
(Columbus)**
Rhodes State Office Tower
30 East Broad Street, 5th Floor
Columbus, OH 43215
614-466-2785
888-278-7101

**Ohio Civil Rights Commission,
Akron Regional Office**
Akron Government Building
161 South High Street, Suite 205
Akron, OH 44308
330-643-3100

**Ohio Civil Rights Commission,
Cincinnati Regional Office**
7162 Reading Road, Suite 1001
Cincinnati, OH 45237
513-852-3344

**Ohio Civil Rights Commission,
Cleveland Regional Office**
615 West Superior Avenue,
Suite 885
Cleveland, OH 44113
216-787-3150

**Ohio Civil Rights Commission,
Columbus Regional Office**
Rhodes State Office Tower
30 East Broad Street, 4th Floor
Columbus, OH 43215
614-466-5928

**Ohio Civil Rights Commission,
Dayton Regional Office**
40 West 4th Street, Suite 1900
Dayton, OH 45402
937-285-6500

**Ohio Civil Rights Commission,
Toledo Regional Office**
One Government Center,
Suite 936
Jackson and Erie Streets
Toledo, OH 43604
419-245-2900
www.state.oh.us/crc

Local Offices of EEOC
Cincinnati Area Office
John W. Peck Federal
Office Building
550 Main Street, Suite 10019
Cincinnati, OH 45202
513-684-2851

Cleveland Field Office
Anthony J. Celebrezze Federal
Building
1240 East 9th Street, Suite
3001
Cleveland, OH 44199
216-522-2001

Detroit Field Office
Patrick V. McNamara Building
477 Michigan Avenue, Room
865
Detroit, MI 48226
800-669-4000

Louisville Area Office
600 Dr. Martin Luther King, Jr.
Place, Suite 268
Louisville, KY 40202
800-669-4000

Philadelphia District Office
801 Market Street, Suite 1300
Philadelphia, PA 19107
215-440-2600

OKLAHOMA

Discrimination/Harassment—
State Agency
**Oklahoma Human Rights
Commission (OHRC),
Oklahoma City Office**
Jim Thorpe Building, Room 480
2101 North Lincoln Boulevard
Oklahoma City, OK 73105
405-521-2360
888-456-2885

**Oklahoma Human Rights
Commission, Tulsa Office**
Kerr Office Building, Room 302

440 South Houston
Tulsa, OK 74127
918-581-2733
888-456-2006
www.hrc.state.ok.us

Local Office of EEOC
Oklahoma City Area Office
215 Dean A McGee Avenue,
5th Floor
Oklahoma City, OK 73102
405-231-4911

OREGON

Discrimination/Harassment—
State Agency
Oregon Bureau of Labor and Industries
Civil Rights Division, Main Office (Portland)
800 Northeast Oregon Street, Suite 1045
Portland, OR 97232
971-673-0761

Oregon Bureau of Labor and Industries
Civil Rights Division, Bend Office
1655 Northeast Forbes Road, Suite 106
Bend, OR 97701
541-322-2435

Oregon Bureau of Labor and Industries
Civil Rights Division, Eugene Office
1400 Executive Parkway, Suite 200
Eugene, OR 97401
541-686-7623

Oregon Bureau of Labor and Industries
Civil Rights Division, Medford Office
119 North Oakdale Avenue
Medford, OR 97501
541-776-6270

Oregon Bureau of Labor and Industries
Civil Rights Division, Pendleton Office
1327 Southeast 3rd Street, Room 110
P.O. Box 459
Pendleton, OR 97801
541-276-7884

Oregon Bureau of Labor and Industries
Civil Rights Division, Salem Office
3865 Wolverine Ave Northeast, Building E, Suite 1
Salem, OR 97305
503-378-3292
www.oregon.gov/BOLI/CRD/about_us.shtml

Local Offices of EEOC
San Francisco District Office
350 The Embarcadero,
Suite 500
San Francisco, CA 94105
415-356-5100

Seattle Field Office
Federal Office Building
909 First Avenue, Suite 400
Seattle, WA 98104
206-220-6883

PENNSYLVANIA

Discrimination/Harassment—
State Agency
**Pennsylvania Human Relations
Commission (PHRC), Central
Office (Harrisburg)**
301 Chestnut Street, Suite 300
Harrisburg, PA 17101
717-787-4410

**Pennsylvania Human Relations
Commission, Harrisburg
Regional Office**
Riverfront Office Center
1101-1125 South Front Street,
5th Floor
Harrisburg, PA 17104
717-787-9784

**Pennsylvania Human Relations
Commission, Philadelphia
Regional Office**
711 State Office Building
1400 Spring Garden Street

Philadelphia, PA 19130
215-560-2496

**Pennsylvania Human Relations
Commission, Pittsburgh
Regional Office**
11th Floor State Office Building
300 Liberty Avenue
Pittsburgh, PA 15222
412-565-5395
www.phrc.state.pa.us

Local Offices of EEOC
Philadelphia District Office
801 Market Street, Suite 1300
Philadelphia, PA 19107
215-440-2600

Pittsburgh Area Office
Liberty Center
1001 Liberty Avenue, Suite 300
Pittsburgh, PA 15222
412-644-3444

RHODE ISLAND

Discrimination/Harassment—
State Agency
Rhode Island Commission for Human Rights
180 Westminster Street, 3rd Floor
Providence, RI 02903
401-222-2661
www.richr.ri.gov

Local Office of EEOC
Boston Area Office
John F. Kennedy Federal Building
475 Government Center
Boston, MA 02203
617-565-3200

SOUTH CAROLINA

Discrimination/Harassment—
State Agency
South Carolina Human Affairs Commission
P.O. Box 4490
2611 Forest Drive, Suite 200
Columbia, SC 29204
803-737-7800, 800-521-0725
www.state.sc.us/schac

Local Offices of EEOC
Charlotte District Office
129 West Trade Street, Suite 400
Charlotte, NC 28202
704-344-6682

Greenville Local Office
301 North Main Street, Suite 1402
Greenville, SC 29601
864-241-4400

Savannah Local Office
410 Mall Boulevard, Suite G
Savannah, GA 31406
912-652-4234

SOUTH DAKOTA

Discrimination/Harassment—
State Agency
**South Dakota Division of
Human Rights**
700 Governors Drive
Pierre, SD 57501
605-773-4493
www.state.sd.us/dcr/hr

Local Office of EEOC
Milwaukee Area Office
Reuss Federal Plaza
310 West Wisconsin Avenue,
Suite 800
Milwaukee, WI 53202
414-297-1111

TENNESSEE

Discrimination/Harassment—
State Agency
**Tennessee Human Rights
Commission (THRC),
Chattanooga Office**
540 McCallie Avenue
4th Floor, West Wing
Chattanooga, TN 37402
423-634-6837

**Tennessee Human Rights
Commission, Knoxville Office**
531 Henley Street, Room 701
Knoxville, TN 37902
865-594-6500

**Tennessee Human Rights
Commission, Memphis Office**
170 North Main Street
State Office Building, 2nd Floor
Memphis, TN 38103
901-543-7389

**Tennessee Human Rights
Commission, Nashville Office**
710 James Robertson Parkway,
Suite 100
Nashville, TN 37243
615-741-5825
800-251-3589
www.tennessee.gov/humanrights

Local Offices of EEOC
Memphis District Office
1407 Union Avenue, Suite 621
Memphis, TN 38104
901-544-0115

Nashville Area Office

50 Vantage Way, Suite 202
Nashville, TN 37228
615-736-5820

TEXAS

Discrimination/Harassment—
State Agency
Texas Workforce Commission
Civil Rights Division
1117 Trinity St, Room 144T
Austin, TX 78778
512463-2642
888-452-4778
www.twc.state.tx.us/customers/
rpm/rpmsubcrd.html

Local Offices of EEOC
Dallas District Office
207 South Houston Street,
3rd Floor
Dallas, TX 75202
214-655-3355

El Paso Area Office
300 East Main Street, Suite 500
El Paso, TX 79901
915-534-6700

Houston District Office
Mickey Leland Federal Building
1919 Smith Street, 6th Floor
Houston, TX 77002
713-209-3320

San Antonio Field Office
Mockingbird Plaza II
5410 Fredericksburg Road,
Suite 200
San Antonio, TX 78229
210-281-7600

UTAH

Discrimination/Harassment—
State Agency
Labor Commission of Utah
Antidiscrimination and
Labor Division
160 East 300 South, 3rd Floor
Salt Lake City, UT 84111
801-530-6801
800-222-1238
http://laborcomission.utah.gov/
AntidiscriminationandLabor/
index.html

Local Office of EEOC
Phoenix District Office
3300 North Central Avenue,
Suite 690
Phoenix, AZ 85012
602-640-5000

VERMONT

Discrimination/Harassment—
State Agency
Attorney General's Office
Civil Rights Division
109 State Street
Montpelier, VT 05609
802-828-3171
www.state.vt.us/atg/civil%20
rights.htm

Local Office of EEOC
Boston Area Office
John F. Kennedy Federal
Building
475 Government Center
Boston, MA 02203
617-565-3200

VIRGINIA

Discrimination/Harassment—
State Agency
Virginia Council on
Human Rights
202 North 9th Street
9th Street Office Building,
11th Floor
Richmond, VA 23219
804-225-2292
www.chr.state.va.us

Local Offices of EEOC
Charlotte District Office
129 West Trade Street, Suite 400
Charlotte, NC 28202
704-344-6682

Norfolk Local Office
Federal Building
200 Granby Street, Suite 739
Norfolk, VA 23510
757-441-3470

Richmond Local Office
830 East Main Street, Suite 600
Richmond, VA 23219
804-278-4651

WASHINGTON

Discrimination/Harassment—
State Agency
Washington State Human
Rights Commission (WSHRC),
Headquarters (Olympia)
711 South Capitol Way, #402
P.O. Box 42490
Olympia, WA 98504
360-753-6770
800-233-3247

Washington State Human
Rights Commission, Seattle
District Office
Melbourne Tower, #921
1511 Third Avenue
Seattle, WA 98101
206-464-6500
800-605-7324

Washington State Human Rights Commission, Spokane District Office
Great Western Building, #416
West 905 Riverside Avenue
Spokane, WA 99201
509-456-4473

Washington State Human Rights Commission, Yakima District Office
Liberty Building, #422
32 North Third Street
Yakima, WA 98901
509-575-2772
800-662-2755
www.hum.wa.gov

Local Office of EEOC
Seattle Field Office
Federal Office Building
909 First Avenue, Suite 400
Seattle, WA 98104
206-220-6883

WASHINGTON, DC

Discrimination/Harassment—
Local Agency
Office of Human Rights
441 4th Street, NW,
Suite 570 North
Washington, DC 20001
202-727-4559
www.ohr.dc.gov/ohr/site/
default.asp

Local Office of EEOC
Washington Field Office
1801 L Street, NW Suite 100
Washington, DC 20507
202-275-7377

WEST VIRGINIA

Discrimination/Harassment—
State Agency
**West Virginia Human Rights
Commission, Main Office
(Charleston)**
1321 Plaza East, Suite 108A
Charleston, WV 25301
304-558-2616
888-676-5546

**West Virginia Human Rights
Commission, Buckhannon
Branch Office**
Route 3, Box 376A
P.O. Box 460
Buckhannon, WV 26201
304-473-4282

**West Virginia Human Rights
Commission, Huntington
Branch Office**
801 Madison Avenue, Suite 233
Huntington, WV 25704
304-528-5823
304-528-5798
www.wvf.state.wv.us/wvhrc

Local Offices of EEOC
Philadelphia District Office
801 Market Street, Suite 1300
Philadelphia, PA 19107
215-440-3600

Pittsburgh Area Office
Liberty Center
1001 Liberty Avenue, Suite 300
Pittsburgh, PA 15222
412-644-3444

WISCONSIN

Discrimination/Harassment—
State Agency
**Wisconsin Equal Rights Division
(WERD), Madison Office**
1 South Pinckney Street,

Room 320
P.O. Box 8928
Madison, WI 53708
608-266-6860

Wisconsin Equal Rights Division, Milwaukee Office
819 North Sixth Street,
Room 255
Milwaukee, WI 53203
414-227-4384
www.dwd.state.wi.us/er

Local Office of EEOC
Milwaukee Area Office
Reuss Federal Plaza
310 West Wisconsin Avenue,
Suite 800
Milwaukee, WI 53203
414-297-1111

WYOMING

Discrimination/Harassment—
State Agency
Wyoming Department of Employment
Labor Standards Division
(WLSD), Casper Office
851 Werner Court, Suite 292
Casper, WY 82601
307-472-3974

Wyoming Department of Employment
Labor Standards Division,
Cheyenne Office
1510 East Pershing Boulevard,
Suite 2015
Cheyenne, WY 82002
307-777-7261

Wyoming Department of Employment
Labor Standards Division,
Salt Lake City Office
10 East South Temple,
Room 1680
Salt Lake City, UT 84133
801-524-5706
http://wydoe.state.wy.us/doe.asp?ID=3

Local Offices of EEOC
Denver Field Office
303 East 17th Avenue,
Suite 510
Denver, CO 80203
303-866-1300

Phoenix District Office
3300 North Central Avenue,
Suite 690
Phoenix, AZ 85012
602-640-5000

Appendix B

DEPARTMENT OF LABOR (DOL), OSHA, AND OTHER GOVERNMENT AGENCIES THAT EMPLOYEES MAY USE BY STATE

This appendix contains a list of state offices for the Department of Labor, OSHA, and other government offices that are part of the Department of Labor. For the federal Department of Labor (DOL) offices, go to www.dol.gov. This federal website is full of great information and is a good place to start.

The list is organized by state name. Even with double- and triple-checking, sometimes a website is closed prior to publication. If the website listed does not work, you can either go to your state's official website—which is usually www.name of the state.gov–or do an Internet search on the state's name plus the words "Department of Labor."

ALABAMA

Alabama Department of Labor
RSA Union, 6th Floor
P.O. Box 303500
Montgomery, AL 36130
334-242-3460
www.alalabor.state.al.us

ESA Wage & Hour Division, Birmingham District Office
Medical Forum Building,
Suite 656
950 22nd Street North
Birmingham, AL 35203
205-731-1305
866-487-9243

ESA Wage & Hour Division, Mobile Area Office
1141 Montlimar Drive
Paramount Center Building,
Suite 1008
Mobile, AL 36609
251-441-5311
866-487-9243

OSHA, Regional Office (Region 4)
61 Forsyth Street, Southwest
Atlanta, GA 30303
404-562-2300

OSHA, Birmingham Area Office
Medical Forum Building
950 22nd Street North
Birmingham, AL 35203
205-731-1534

OSHA, Mobile Area Office
1141 Montlimar Drive,
Suite 1008
Mobile, AL 36609
251-441-6131

ALASKA

Alaska Department of Labor &
Workforce Development
111 West 8th Street, Room 304
Juneau, AK 99801
907-465-2700
http://labor.state.ak.us/

**OSHA, Regional Office
(Region 10)**
1111 Third Avenue, Suite 715

Seattle, WA 98101
206-553-5930

OSHA, Anchorage Area Office
222 West 7th Avenue,
Room A14
Anchorage, AK 99513
907-271-5152

ARIZONA

**Industrial Commission of
Arizona
Department of Labor,
Phoenix Office**
800 West Washington Street
Phoenix, AZ 85007
602-542-4515

**Industrial Commission of
Arizona
Department of Labor,
Tucson Office**
2675 East Broadway
Tucson, AZ 85716
520-628-5459
www.ica.state.az.us

**ESA Wage & Hour Division,
Phoenix District Office**
230 North First Avenue,
Suite 402
Phoenix, AZ 85003
602-514-7100

**OSHA, Regional Office
(Region 9)**
90 7th Street, Suite 18100
San Francisco, CA 94103
415-625-2547

Arizona Division of
Occupational Safety and
Health, Phoenix Office
800 West Washington Street,
2nd Floor
Phoenix, AZ 85007
602-542-5795

Arizona Division of
Occupational Safety and
Health, Tucson Office
2657 East Broadway
Boulevard #239
Tucson, AZ 85716
520-628-5478

ARKANSAS

Arkansas Department of Labor
Labor Standards Division
10421 West Markham
Little Rock, Arkansas 72205
501-682-4500
www.accessarkansas.org/labor/
index.html

**ESA Wage & Hour Division,
Little Rock Office**
Danville Building 2, Suite 220
10810 Executive Center Drive
Little Rock, AR 72221
501-223-9114

**OSHA, Regional Office
(Region 6)**
525 Griffin Street, Room 602
Dallas, TX 75202
972-850-4145

**OSHA, Area Office,
Little Rock Area Office**
10810 Executive Center Drive
Danville Bldg #2, Suite 206
Little Rock, AR 72211
501-224-1841

CALIFORNIA

Department of Industrial Relations
Division of Occupational Safety and Health
455 Golden Gate Avenue
San Francisco, CA 94102
415-703-5050
www.dir.ca.gov/occupational_safety.html

ESA Wage & Hour Division, East Los Angeles Office
100 North Barranca Street, Suite 850
West Covina, CA 91791
626-966-0478

ESA Wage & Hour Division, Los Angeles Office
915 Wilshire Boulevard, Suite 960
Los Angeles, CA 90017
213-894-6375

ESA Wage & Hour Division, Orange Area Office
770 The City Drive South, Suite 5710
Orange, CA 92868
714-621-1650

ESA Wage & Hour Division, Sacramento Office
2800 Cottage Way, Room W-1836
Sacramento, CA 95825
916-978-6123

ESA Wage & Hour Division, San Diego Office
5675 Ruffin Road, Suite 310
San Diego, CA 92123
858-467-7015

ESA Wage & Hour Division, San Francisco Office
90 7th Street, Suite 18-300
San Francisco, CA 94103
415-625-7720

ESA Wage & Hour Division, San Jose Area Office
60 South Market Street, Suite 420
San Jose, CA 95113
408-291-7730

OSHA, Regional Office (Region 9)
90 7th Street, Suite 18100
San Francisco, CA 94103
415-625-2547

COLORADO

Colorado Department of Labor and Employment
633 17th Street, Suite 200
Denver, CO 80202
303-318-8441
www.coworkforce.com

ESA Wage & Hour Division, Denver District Office
1999 Broadway, Suite 2445
Denver, CO 80202
720-264-3250

OSHA, Regional Office (Region 8)
1999 Broadway, Suite 1690
Denver, CO 80202
720-264-6550

OSHA, Denver Area Office
1391 Speer Boulevard, Suite 210
Denver, CO 80204
303-844-5285

OSHA, Englewood Area Office
7935 East Prentice Avenue, Suite 209
Englewood, CO 80111
303-843-4500

CONNECTICUT

Connecticut Department of Labor
200 Folly Brook Boulevard
Wethersfield, CT 06109
860-263-6000
www.ctdol.state.ct.us/index.htm

ESA Wage & Hour Division, Hartford District Office
135 High Street, Room 210
Hartford, CT 06103
860-240-4160

ESA Wage & Hour Division,
New Haven Area Office
150 Court Street, Room 423
New Haven, CT 06510
203-773-2249

OSHA, Bridgeport Area Office
Clark Building
1057 Broad Street, 4th Floor
Bridgeport, CT 06604
203-579-5581

OSHA, Regional Office
(Region 1)
JFK Federal Building, Room
E340
Boston, MA 02203
617-565-9860

OSHA, Hartford Area Office
Federal Building
450 Main Street, Room 613
Hartford, CT 06103
860-240-3152

DELAWARE

Delaware Department of Labor
Division of Industrial Affairs,
Wilmington Office
4425 North Market Street,
3rd Floor
Wilmington, DE 19802
302-761-8200

ESA Wage & Hour Division,
Baltimore, MD District Office
Appraisers Stores Building
103 South Gay Street,
Room 207
Baltimore, MD 21202
410-962-6211

Division of Industrial Affairs,
Milford Office
13 Northwest Front Street,
Suite 100
Milford, DE 19963
302-422-1134
www.delawareworks.com

OSHA, Regional Office
(Region 3)
The Curtis Center,
Suite 740 West
170 South Independence
Mall West
Philadelphia, PA 19106
215-861-4900

OSHA, Wilmington Area Office
Mellon Bank Building, Suite 900
919 Market Street
Wilmington, DE 19801
302-573-6518

FLORIDA

**ESA Wage & Hour Division,
Fort Lauderdale Area Office**
Federal Building, Room 408
299 East Broward Boulevard
Fort Lauderdale, FL 33301
954-356-6896

**ESA Wage & Hour Division,
Jacksonville District Office**
Charles E. Bennett Federal
Building
400 West Bay Street, Room 956
Jacksonville, FL 32202
(904) 359-9292

**ESA Wage & Hour Division,
Miami District Office**
Sunset Center, Room 255
10300 Sunset Drive
Miami, FL 33173
305-598-6607

**ESA Wage & Hour Division,
Orlando Area Office**
1001 Executive Center
Drive #103
Orlando, FL 32803
407-648-6471

**ESA Wage & Hour Division,
Tallahassee Area Office**
227 North Bronough Street,
Room 4120
Tallahassee, FL 32301
850-942-8341

**ESA Wage & Hour Division,
Tampa District Office**
Austin Laurel Building
4905 West Laurel Avenue,
Suite 300
Tampa, FL 33607813-288-1242

OSHA, Regional Office (Region 4)
61 Forsyth Street, Southwest
Atlanta, GA 30303
404-562-2300

OSHA, Fort Lauderdale Area Office
8040 Peters Road, Building H-100
Fort Lauderdale, FL 33324
954-424-0242

OSHA, Jacksonville Area Office
Ribault Building, Suite 227
1851 Executive Center Drive
Jacksonville, FL 32207
904-232-2895

OSHA, Tampa Area Office
5807 Breckenridge Parkway, Suite A
Tampa, FL 33610
813-626-1177

GEORGIA

ESA Wage & Hour Division, Atlanta District Office
61 Forsyth Street, Southwest, Room 7M10
Atlanta, GA 30303
404-893-4600

ESA Wage & Hour Division, Savannah Area Office
Juliette Gordon Low Federal Bldg. Complex
124 Barnard Street, Suite B-210
Savannah, GA 31401
912-652-4221

OSHA, Regional Office (Region 4)
61 Forsyth Street, Southwest
Atlanta, GA 30303
404-562-2300

OSHA, Atlanta East Area Office
LaVista Perimeter Office Park
2183 North Lake Parkway, Building 7, Suite 110
Tucker, GA 30084
770-493-6644

OSHA, Atlanta West Area Office
2400 Herodian Way, Suite 250
Smyrna, GA 30080
770-984-8700

OSHA, Savannah Area Office
450 Mall Boulevard, Suite J
Savannah, GA 31406
912-652-4393

HAWAII

Department of Labor and Industrial Relations
830 Punchbowl Street, Room 321
Honolulu, HI 96813
808-586-8844
http://hawaii.gov/labor/

OSHA, Regional Office (Region 9)
90 7th Street, Suite 18100
San Francisco, CA 94103
415-625-2547

ESA Wage & Hour Division, Honolulu Area Office
300 Ala Moana Blvd, Room 7225
Honolulu, HI 96850
808-541-1361

IDAHO

Idaho Department of Labor
317 West Main Street
Boise, ID 83735-0001
(208) 3342-3570
http://labor.idaho.gov

ESA Wage & Hour Division, Seattle, WA District Office
(Serves Northern Panhandle—Benewah, Bonner, Boundary, Clearwater, Idaho, Kootenai, Latah, Lewis, Nez Perce, and Shoshone Counties)

1111 Third Avenue, Suite 755
Seattle, WA 98101
206-398-8039

**ESA Wage & Hour Division,
Portland, OR District Office**
(Serves remainder of state)
620 Southwest Main Street,
Room 423
Portland, OR 97205
503-326-3057

**OSHA, Regional Office
(Region 10)**
1111 Third Avenue, Suite 715
Seattle, WA 98101
206-553-5930

OSHA, Boise Area Office
1150 North Curtis Road, Suite
201
Boise, ID 83706
208-321-2960

ILLINOIS

**Illinois Department of Labor,
Chicago Office**
160 North LaSalle, Suite
C-1300
Chicago, IL 60601
312-793-2800

**Illinois Department of Labor,
Marion Office**
2309 West Main Street, Suite 115
Marion, IL 62959
618-993-7090
www.state.il.us/agency/idol

**Illinois Department of Labor,
Springfield Office**
1 West Old State Capitol Plaza,
Room 300
Springfield, IL 62701
217-782-6206

**ESA Wage & Hour Division,
Chicago District Office**
230 South Dearborn Street,
Room 412
Chicago, IL 60604
312-596-7230

ESA Wage & Hour Division, Springfield Area Office
3160 West White Oaks Drive, Suite 203
Springfield, IL 62704
217-793-5028

ESA Wage & Hour Division, St. Louis, MO District Office
(Serves Calhoun, Jersey, Madison, Monroe, Randolph, and St. Clair counties)
1222 Spruce Street, Room 9.102B
St. Louis, MO 63103
314-539-2706

OSHA, Regional Office (Region 5)
230 South Dearborn Street, Room 3244
Chicago, IL 60604
312-353-2220

OSHA, Calumet City Area Office
1600 167th Street, Suite 9
Calumet City, IL 60409
708-891-3800

OSHA, Chicago North Area Office
701 Lee Street, Suite 950
Des Plaines, IL 60016
847-803-4800

OSHA, Fairview Heights District Office
11 Executive Drive, Suite 11
Fairview Heights, IL 62208
618-632-8612

OSHA, North Aurora Area Office
365 Smoke Tree Plaza
North Aurora, IL 60542
630-896-8700

OSHA, Peoria Area Office
2918 West Willows Knolls Road
Peoria, IL 61614
309-589-7033

INDIANA

Indiana Department of Labor
402 West Washington Street,
Room W-195
Indianapolis, IN 46204
317-232-2655
www.in.gov/dol

**ESA Wage & Hour Division,
Indianapolis District Office**
46 East Ohio Street, Room 413
Indianapolis, IN 46204
317-226-6801

**ESA Wage & Hour Division,
South Bend Area Office**
2420 Viridian Drive, Suite 160
South Bend, IN 46628
574-236-8331

**OSHA, Regional Office
(Region 5)**
230 South Dearborn Street,
Room 3244
Chicago, IL 60604
312-353-2220

**OSHA, Indianapolis Area
Office**
46 East Ohio Street,
Room 423
Indianapolis, IN 46204
317-226-7290

IOWA

Iowa Division of Labor Services
1000 East Grand Avenue
Des Moines, IA 50319
515-242-5870

**ESA Wage & Hour Division,
Des Moines District Office**
Federal Building
210 Walnut Street, Room 643
Des Moines, IA 50309
515-284-4625

U.S. Department of Labor Occupational Safety and Health Administration
210 Walnut Street, Room 815
Des Moines, IA 50309
515-284-4794
www.iowaworkforce.org/labor/
iosh/index.html

OSHA, Regional Office (Region 7)
Two Pershing Square
2300 Main Street, Suite 1010
Kansas City, MO 64108
816-283-8745

KANSAS

Kansas Department of Labor
401 Southwest Topeka
Boulevard
Topeka, KS 66603
785-296-5000
www.dol.ks.gov/index.html

OSHA, Regional Office (Region 7)
Two Pershing Square
2300 Main Street, Suite 1010
Kansas City, MO 64108
816-283-8745

ESA Wage & Hour Division, Kansas City District Office
Gateway Tower II
350 State Avenue, Suite 1010
Kansas City, KS 66101
913-551-5721

OSHA, Wichita Area Office
271 West 3rd Street North,
Room 400
Wichita, KS 67202
316-269-6644

KENTUCKY

Kentucky Labor Cabinet
1047 U.S. Highway
127 South, Suite 4
Frankfort, KY 40601
502-564-3070
www.labor.ky.gov

**OSHA, Regional Office
(Region 4)**
61 Forsyth Street,
Southwest
Atlanta, GA 30303
404-562-2300

**ESA Wage & Hour Division,
Louisville District Office**
Gene Snyder U.S. Courthouse
and Customhouse
601 West Broadway, Room 31
Louisville, KY 40202
502-582-5226

OSHA, Frankfort Area Office
330 West Broadway,
Room 108
Frankfort, KY 40601
502-227-7024

LOUISIANA

**ESA Wage & Hour Division,
New Orleans District Office**
600 South Maestri Place,
Room 615
New Orleans, LA 70130504-
589-6171

**OSHA, Baton Rouge
Area Office**
9100 Bluebonnet Centre
Boulevard, Suite 201
Baton Rouge, LA 70809
225-298-5458

**OSHA, Regional Office
(Region 6)**
525 Griffin Street, Room 602
Dallas, TX 75202
972-850-4145

MAINE

Department of Labor
45 Commerce Drive
Augusta, ME 04333
207-623-7900
www.maine.gov/labor

OSHA, Augusta Area Office
40 Western Avenue,
Room G-26
Augusta, ME 04330
207-626-9160

ESA Wage & Hour Division,
Manchester, NH District Office
1750 Elm Street, Suite 111
Manchester, NH 03104
603-666-7716

OSHA, Bangor Area Office
202 Harlow Street,
Room 211
Bangor, ME 04401
207-941-8177

OSHA, Regional Office
(Region 1)
JFK Federal Building,
Room E340
Boston, MA 02203
617-565-9860

MARYLAND

Department of Labor, Licensing
& Regulation
500 North Calvert Street #401
Baltimore, MD 21202
410-230-6001
www.dllr.state.md.us/index.html

ESA Wage & Hour Division,
Baltimore District Office
Appraisers Stores Building
103 South Gay Street,
Room 207
Baltimore, MD 21202
410-962-6211

OSHA, Regional Office (Region 3)
The Curtis Center,
Suite 740 West
170 South Independence Mall West
Philadelphia, PA 19106
215-861-4900

Maryland Occupational Safety and Health
1100 Eutaw Street, Room 613
Baltimore, MD 21202
410-767-2190

OSHA, Baltimore/Washington Area Office
1099 Winterson Road, Suite 140
Linthicum, MD 21090
410-865-2055

MASSACHUSETTS

Department of Labor
1 Ashburton Place, Room 2112
Boston, MA 02108
www.mass.gov

ESA Wage & Hour Division, Boston District Office
John F. Kennedy Federal Building, Room 525
Boston, MA 02203
617-624-6700

ESA Wage & Hour Division, Taunton Area Office
17 Broadway, Room 308
Taunton, MA 02780
508-821-9106

OSHA, Regional Office (Region 1)
JFK Federal Building, Room E340
Boston, MA 02203
617-565-9860

OSHA, North Boston Area Office
Valley Office Park
13 Branch Street
Methuen, MA 01844
617-565-8110

OSHA, South Boston Area Office
639 Granite Street, 4th Floor
Braintree, MA 02184
617-565-6923

OSHA, Springfield Area Office
1441 Main Street, Room 550
Springfield, Massachusetts
01103-1493
413-785-0136

MICHIGAN

Department of Labor and Economic Growth
Wage & Hour Division, Lansing Office
6546 Mercantile Way, Suite 5
Lansing, MI 48909
517-335-0400

Wage & Hour Division, Livonia Office
33523 West 9 Mile Road, B1
Livonia, MI 48152
313-456-4906
www.michigan.gov/dleg

ESA Wage & Hour Division, Detroit District Office
211 West Fort Street Room, 1317
Detroit, MI 48226
313-226-7448

ESA Wage & Hour Division, Grand Rapids Area Office
800 Monroe Avenue, Northwest, Suite 315
Grand Rapids, MI 49503
616-456-2004

OSHA, Regional Office (Region 5)
230 South Dearborn Street, Room 3244
Chicago, IL 60604
312-353-2220

Michigan Occupational Safety & Health Administration
7150 Harris Drive
Lansing, MI 48909
517-322-1817

OSHA, Lansing Area Office
315 West Allegan, Room 207
Lansing, MI 48933
517-487-4996

MINNESOTA

Minnesota Department of Labor and Industry
443 Lafayette Road North
St. Paul, MN 55155
651-284-5070, 800-342-5354
www.doli.state.mn.us/
laborlaw.html

ESA Wage & Hour Division, Minneapolis District Office
Midland Square, Suite 920
331 Second Avenue South
Minneapolis, MN 55401
612-370-3371

OSHA, Regional Office (Region 5)
230 South Dearborn Street,
Room 3244
Chicago, IL 60604
312-353-2220

OSHA, Eau Claire Area Office
1310 West Clairemont Avenue
Eau Claire, WI 54701
715-832-1147

MISSISSIPPI

ESA Wage & Hour Division, Birmingham, AL District Office
(Serves Northeast Quadrant)
Medical Forum Building,
Suite 656
950 22nd Street North
Birmingham, AL 35203
205-731-1305
866-487-9243

ESA Wage & Hour Division, Jackson Area Office
McCoy Federal Building
100 West Capitol Street,
Suite 608
Jackson, MS 39269
601-965-4347

OSHA, Regional Office (Region 4)
61 Forsyth Street, Southwest
Atlanta, GA 30303
404-562-2300

OSHA, Jackson Area Office
3780 I-55 North, Suite 210
Jackson, MS 39211
601-965-4606

MISSOURI

Department of Labor
Division of Labor Standards
3315 West Truman Boulevard,
Room 205
Jefferson City, MO 65102
573-751-3403
www.dolir.mo.gov

ESA Wage & Hour Division, St. Louis District Office
(Serves the eastern half of Missouri)
1222 Spruce Street, Room 9.102B
St. Louis, MO 63101
314-539-2706

ESA Wage & Hour Division, Kansas City, KS District Office
(Services the western half of Missouri)
Gateway Tower II

400 State Avenue, Suite 1010
Kansas City, KS 66101
913-551-5721

OSHA, Regional Office (Region 7)
Two Pershing Square
2300 Main Street, Suite 1010
Kansas City, MO 64108
816-283-8745

OSHA, Kansas City Area Office
6200 Connecticut Avenue, Suite 100
Kansas City, MO 64120
816-483-9531

OSHA, St. Louis Area Office
911 Washington Avenue, Room 420
St. Louis, MO 63101
314-425-4249

MONTANA

Montana Department of Labor and Industry
P.O. Box 1729
Helena, MT 59624
406-444-2840
http://dli.mt.gov/

ESA Wage & Hour Division, Salt Lake City, UT District Office
10 East South Temple, Suite 1680
Salt Lake City, UT 84133
801-524-5706

OSHA, Regional Office (Region 8)
1999 Broadway, Suite 1690
Denver, CO 80202
720-264-6550

OSHA, Billings Area Office
2900 4th Avenue North, Suite 303
Billings, MT 59101
406-247-7494

NEBRASKA

**Nebraska Workforce Development
Nebraska Department of Labor, Lincoln Office**
301 Centennial Mall South
Lincoln, NE 68509
402-471-2239

Nebraska Department of Labor, Omaha Offices
5723 F Street, 2nd Floor
Omaha, NE 68117
402-595-3095
www.dol.state.ne.us

State Office Building
5404 Cedar St., 3rd Floor
Omaha, NE 68106-2365
(402) 595-3095

Nebraska Department of Labor Division of Safety and Labor Standards
301 Centennial Mall South, LL
P.O. Box 95024
Lincoln, NE 68509-5024
(402) 471-2239

ESA Wage & Hour Division Omaha Area Office
111 South 18th Plaza,
Suite 2238
Omaha, NE 68102-1615
(402) 221-4682

OSHA, Regional Office (Region 7)
Two Pershing Square
2300 Main Street, Suite 1010
Kansas City, MO 64108
816-283-8745

OSHA, Omaha Area Office
Overland-Wolf Building
6910 Pacific Street, Room 100
Omaha, NE 68106
402-553-0171

NEVADA

Office of the Labor Commissioner, Carson City Office
675 Fairview Drive, Suite 226
Carson City, NV 89701
775-687-4850
www.laborcommissioner.com

Office of the Labor Commissioner, Las Vegas Office
555 East Washington Avenue,
Suite 4100
Las Vegas, NV 89101
702-486-2650

ESA Wage & Hour Division, Phoenix, AZ District Office
(Serves Clark, Lincoln, and Nye Counties)
230 North First Avenue, Suite 402
Phoenix, AZ 85003
602-514-7100

ESA Wage & Hour Division, Sacramento, CA District Office
(Serves remainder of state)
2800 Cottage Way,
Room W-1836
Sacramento, CA 95825-1886
916-978-6123

OSHA, Regional Office (Region 9)
90 7th Street, Suite 18100
San Francisco, CA 94103
415-625-2547

OSHA, Nevada Office
1301 North Green Valley Parkway, Suite 200
Henderson, NV 89074
702-486-9020

NEW HAMPSHIRE

New Hampshire Department of Labor
95 Pleasant Street
Concord, NH 03301
603-271-3176
www.labor.state.nh.us/default.asp

ESA Wage & Hour Division, Manchester District Office
1750 Elm Street, Suite 111
Manchester, NH 03104
603-666-7716

OSHA, Regional Office (Region 1)
JFK Federal Building,
Room E340
Boston, MA 02203
617-565-9860

OSHA, Concord Area Office
53 Pleasant Street, Room 3901
Concord, NH 03301
603-225-1629

NEW JERSEY

New Jersey Department of Labor and Workforce Development Division of Wage and Hour Compliance
One John Fitch Plaza, 3rd Floor
Trenton, NJ 08611
609-292-2305
http://lwd.dol.state.nj.us/labor/wagehour/wagehour_index.html

ESA Wage & Hour Division, Northern New Jersey District Office
200 Sheffield Street, Room 102
Mountainside, NJ 07092
973-645-2279

ESA Wage & Hour Division, Southern New Jersey District Office
3131 Princeton Pike, Building 5, Room 216
Lawrenceville, NJ 08648
609-538-8310

OSHA, Regional Office (Region 2)
201 Varick Street, Room 670
New York, NY 10014
212-337-2378

New Jersey Department of Labor and Workforce Development Public Employees Occupational Safety and Health Office
One John Fitch Plaza
Trenton, NJ 08625
609-633-3896

OSHA, Avenel Area Office
1030 St. Georges Avenue
Plaza 35, Suite 205
Avenel, NJ 07001
732-750-3270

OSHA, Hasbrouck Heights Area Office
500 Route 17 South,
2nd Floor
Hasbrouck Heights,
NJ 07604
201-288-1700

OSHA, Marlton Area Office
Marlton Executive Park,
Building 2
701 Route 73 South,
Suite 120
Marlton, NJ 08053
856-396-2594

OSHA, Parsippany Area Office
299 Cherry Hill Road,
Suite 103
Parsippany, NJ 07054
973-263-1003

NEW MEXICO

New Mexico Department of Workforce Solutions
Wage & Hour Bureau, Albuquerque Office
625 Silver Avenue Southwest
Albuquerque, NM 87102
505-841-4400

Wage & Hour Bureau, Las Cruces Office
506 South Main, Suite 10200
Las Cruces, NM 88001
575-524-6195

Wage & Hour Bureau, Santa Fe Office
1596 Pacheco Street, Suite 201
Santa Fe, NM 87505
505-827-6838
www.dws.state.nm.us/
dws-wagehour.html

ESA Wage & Hour Division, Albuquerque District Office
Western Bank Building
500 Fourth Street, Suite 403
Albuquerque, NM 87102
505-245-2142

OSHA, Regional Office (Region 6)
525 Griffin Street, Room 602
Dallas, TX 75202
972-850-4145

OSHA, Lubbock Area Office
1205 Texas Avenue, Room 806
Lubbock, TX 79401
806-472-7681

NEW YORK

New York Department of Labor
W. Averell Harriman State
Office Campus
Building 12
Albany, NY 12240
518-457-9000
www.labor.state.ny.us/wage-sandhours.shtm

**ESA Wage & Hour Division,
Albany District Office**
Leo W. O'Brien Federal Building
Room 822
Albany, NY 12207
518-431-4278

**ESA Wage & Hour Division,
Brooklyn Area Office**
625 Fulton Street, 7th Floor
Brooklyn, NY 11201
718-254-9410

**ESA Wage & Hour Division,
Buffalo Area Office**
130 South Elmwood Avenue,
Room 534
Buffalo, NY 14202
585-263-6283

**ESA Wage & Hour Division,
Hudson Valley Area Office**
140 Grand Street, Suite 304
White Plains, NY 10601
914-682-6348

**ESA Wage & Hour Division,
Long Island District Office**
1400 Old Country Road,
Suite 410
Westbury, NY 11590
516-338-1890

**ESA Wage & Hour Division,
New York City District Office**
26 Federal Plaza, Room 3700
New York, NY 10278
212-264-8185

**ESA Wage & Hour Division,
Syracuse Area Office**
100 South Clinton Street,
FOB Room 1373
Syracuse, NY 13261
315-448-0630

OSHA, Regional Office (Region 2)
201 Varick Street, Room 670
New York, NY 10014
212-337-2378

OSHA, Albany Area Office
401 New Karner Road, Suite 300
Albany, NY 12205
518-464-4338

OSHA, Bayside District Office of the Long Island Area Office
42-40 Bell Boulevard
Bayside, NY 11361(718) 279-9060

OSHA, Buffalo Area Office
130 South Elmwood Avenue, Suite 500
Buffalo, NY 14202
716-551-3053

OSHA, Long Island Area Office
1400 Old Country Road, Suite 208
Westbury, NY 11590
516-334-3344

OSHA, Manhattan Area Office
201 Varick Street Room 908
New York, NY 10014
212-620-3200

OSHA, Queens District Office of the Manhattan Area Office
45-17 Marathon Parkway
Little Neck, NY 11362
718-279-9060

OSHA, Syracuse Area Office
3300 Vickery Road
North Syracuse, NY 13212
315-451-0808

OSHA, Tarrytown Area Office
660 White Plains Road, 4th Floor
Tarrytown, NY 10591
914-524-7510

NORTH CAROLINA

North Carolina Department of Labor
Wage and Hour Bureau
4 West Edenton Street
Raleigh, NC 27601
919-807-2796
www.nclabor.com/wh/wh.htm

ESA Wage & Hour Division, Charlotte District Office
3800 Arco Corporate Drive, Suite 460
Charlotte, NC 28273
704-749-3360

ESA Wage & Hour Division, Raleigh District Office
Somerset Bank Building
4407 Bland Road, Suite 260
Raleigh, NC 27609
919-790-2741

OSHA, Regional Office (Region 4)
61 Forsyth Street, Southwest
Atlanta, GA 30303
404-562-2300

OSHA, Raleigh Area Office
4407 Bland Road, Suite 210
Raleigh, NC 27609
919-790-8096

North Carolina Department of Labor
Occupational Safety and Health Division
111 Hillborough Street
Raleigh, NC 27601
919-733-7166

NORTH DAKOTA

North Dakota Department of Labor
Wage & Hour Division
State Capitol, 13th Floor
Bismarck, ND 58505
701-328-2660
www.state.nd.us/labor/services/
wage-hour

ESA Wage & Hour Division, Denver, CO District Office
1999 Broadway, Suite 2445
Denver, CO 80202
720-264-3250

OSHA, Regional Office (Region 8)
1999 Broadway, Suite 1690
Denver, CO 80202
720-264-6550

OSHA, Bismarck Area Office
Federal Office Building
1640 East Capitol Avenue
Bismarck, ND 58501
701-250-4521

OHIO

Division of Labor and Worker Safety
Wage and Hour Bureau
77 South High Street, 22nd Floor
Columbus, OH 43215
614-644-2239
www.com.ohio.gov/laws

ESA Wage & Hour Division, Cincinnati Area Office
550 Main Street, Room 10-409
Cincinnati, OH 45202
513-684-2908

ESA Wage & Hour Division, Cleveland District Office
Federal Office Building
1240 East 9th Street, Room 817
Cleveland, OH 44199
216-357-5400

ESA Wage & Hour Division, Columbus District Office
200 North High, Room 646
Columbus, OH 43215
614-469-5677

OSHA, Regional Office (Region 5)
230 South Dearborn Street, Room 3244
Chicago, IL 60604
312-353-2220

OSHA, Cincinnati Area Office
36 Triangle Park Drive
Cincinnati, OH 45246
513-841-4132

OSHA, Cleveland Area Office
Federal Office Building
1240 East 9th Street, Room 899
Cleveland, OH 44199
216-615-4266

OSHA, Columbus Area Office
Federal Office Building
200 North High Street, Room 620
Columbus, OH 43215
614-469-5582

OSHA, Toledo Area Office
Ohio Building
420 Madison Avenue, Suite 600
Toledo, OH 43604
419-259-7542

OKLAHOMA

Oklahoma Department of Labor Wage & Hour Division, Oklahoma City Office
4001 North Lincoln Blvd.
Oklahoma City, OK 73105
405-528-1500

Wage & Hour Division, Tulsa Office
440 South Houston, Suite 300
Tulsa, OK 74127
918-581-2400
www.ok.gov/odol

ESA Wage & Hour Division, Little Rock, AR District Office
Danville Building 2, Suite 220
10810 Executive Center Drive
Little Rock, AR 72221
501-223-9114

OSHA, Regional Office (Region 6)
525 Griffin Street, Room 602
Dallas, TX 75202
972-850-4145

OSHA, Oklahoma City Area Office
55 North Robinson, Suite 315
Oklahoma City, OK 73102
405-278-9560

OREGON

Bureau of Labor and Industries
800 Northeast Oregon Street, Suite 1045
Portland, OR 97232
971-673-0761
www.oregon.com/boli

ESA Wage & Hour Division, Portland District Office
620 Southwest Main Street, Room 423
Portland, OR 97205
503-326-3057

OSHA, Regional Office (Region 10)
1111 Third Avenue, Suite 715
Seattle, Washington 98101-3212
206-553-5930

Oregon OSHA
Salem Central Office
350 Winter Street, Northeast, Room 430
Salem, OR 97309
503-378-3272

OSHA, Portland Area Office
1220 Southwest 3rd Avenue,
Room 640
Portland, OR 97204
503-326-2251

PENNSYLVANIA

Department of Labor and Industry
7th and Forster Streets
Harrisburg, PA 17120
717-787-5279
www.dli.state.pa.us/landi/cwp/
view.asp?a=196&Q=65894&lan
diRNavradC6865=|

ESA Wage & Hour Division, Philadelphia District Office
U.S. Custom House, Room 400
Second & Chestnut Streets
Philadelphia, PA 19106
215-597-4950

ESA Wage & Hour Division, Pittsburgh District Office
Federal Building
1000 Liberty Avenue, Suite 1416
Pittsburgh, PA 15222
412-395-4996

ESA Wage & Hour Division, Wilkes Barre District Office
7 North Wilkes-Barre Boulevard
Stegmaier Building, Suite 373M
Wilkes Barre, PA 18702
570-826-6316

OSHA, Regional Office (Region 3)
The Curtis Center,
Suite 740 West
170 South Independence
Mall West
Philadelphia, PA 19106
215-861-4900

OSHA, Allentown Area Office
850 North 5th Street
Allentown, PA 18102
610-776-0592

OSHA, Erie Area Office
1128 State Street, Suite 200
Erie, PA 16501
814-461-1492

OSHA, Harrisburg Area Office
Progress Plaza
49 North Progress Avenue
Harrisburg, PA 17109
717-782-3902

OSHA, Philadelphia Area Office
U.S. Custom House, Room 242
Second & Chestnut Street
Philadelphia, PA 19106
215-597-4955

OSHA, Pittsburgh Area Office
1000 Liberty Avenue,
Room 905
Pittsburgh, PA 15222
412-395-4903

OSHA, Wilkes-Barre Area Office
The Stegmaier Building,
Suite 410
7 North Wilkes-Barre Boulevard
Wilkes-Barre, PA 18702
570-826-6538

RHODE ISLAND

ESA Wage & Hour Division, Providence Area Office
380 Westminster Mall, Room 546
Providence, RI 02903
401-528-4431

OSHA, Regional Office (Region 1)
JFK Federal Building, Room E340
Boston, MA 02203
617-565-9860

OSHA, Providence Area Office
Federal Office Building
380 Westminster Mall,
Room 543
Providence, RI 02903
401-528-4669

SOUTH CAROLINA

**South Carolina Department of
Labor
Office of Wages and Child Labor**
110 Centerview Drive
Columbia, SC 29211
803-896-4840
www.llr.state.sc.us/Labor

**ESA Wage & Hour Division,
Columbia District Office**
Federal Building, Room 1072
1835 Assembly Street
Columbia, SC 29201
803-765-5981

**OSHA, Regional Office
(Region 4)**
61 Forsyth Street, Southwest
Atlanta, GA 30303
404-562-2300

OSHA, Columbia Area Office
1835 Assembly Street,
Room 1472
Columbia, SC 29201
803-765-5904

**South Carolina
Department of Labor
Division of Occupational
Safety and Health**
3600 Forest Drive
Columbia, SC 29211
803-896-7665

SOUTH DAKOTA

**South Dakota Department of
Labor
Division of Labor & Management**
Kneip Building
700 Governors Drive
Pierre, SD 57501

605-773-3681
http://dol.sd.gov/wagehrs/
default.aspx

ESA Wage & Hour Division, Denver, CO District Office
1999 Broadway, Suite 2445
Denver, CO 80202
720-264-3250

OSHA, Regional Office (Region 8)
1999 Broadway, Suite 1690
Denver, CO 80202
720-264-6550

TENNESSEE

Tennessee Department of Labor and Workforce Development
220 French Landing Drive
Nashville, TN 37243
615-741-6642
http://www.state.tn.us/labor-wfd/lsdiv.html

ESA Wage & Hour Division, Nashville District Office
1321 Murfreesboro Road, Suite 511
Nashville, TN 37217
615-781-5344

ESA Wage & Hour Division, Knoxville Area Office
John J. Duncan Federal Building
710 Locust Street, Room 101
Knoxville, TN 37902
865-545-4619

ESA Wage & Hour Division, Memphis Area Office
Federal Office Building
167 North Main Street, Room 484
Memphis, TN 38103
901-544-3418

OSHA, Regional Office (Region 4)
61 Forsyth Street, Southwest
Atlanta, GA 30303
404-562-2300

OSHA, Nashville Area Office
51 Century Boulevard, Suite 340
Nashville, TN 37214
615-232-3803

TEXAS

Texas Workforce Commission
101 East 15th Street
Austin, TX 78778
512-837-9559
www.twc.state.tx.us

ESA Wage & Hour Division,
Dallas District Office
The Offices at Brookhollow
1701 East Lamar Boulevard,
Suite 270
Arlington, TX 76006
817-861-2150

ESA Wage & Hour Division,
Houston District Office
8701 South Gessner Drive,
Suite 1164
Houston, TX 77044
713-339-5525

ESA Wage & Hour Division,
San Antonio District Office
Northchase 1 Office Building
10127 Morocco, Suite 140
San Antonio, TX 78216
713-339-4400

ESA Wage & Hour Division,
Albuquerque District Office
(Serves West Texas Panhandle
and Northwest Quadrant)
Western Bank Building
500 Fourth Street, Suite 840
Albuquerque, NM 87102
505-245-2142

OSHA, Regional Office
(Region 6)
525 Griffin Street, Room 602
Dallas, TX 75202
972-850-4145

OSHA, Austin Area Office
1033 La Posada Drive, Suite 375
Austin, TX 78752
512-374-0271

OSHA, Corpus Christi
Area Office
Wilson Plaza, Suite 700
606 North Carancahua
Corpus Christi, TX 78476
361-888-3420

OSHA, Dallas Area Office
8344 East RL Thornton
Freeway, Suite 420
Dallas, TX 75228
214-320-2400

OSHA, El Paso District Office
4849 North Mesa Street,
Suite 200
El Paso, TX 79912
915-534-6251

OSHA, Fort Worth Area Office
8713 Airport Freeway, Suite 302
Fort Worth, TX 76180
817-428-2470

**OSHA, Houston North
Area Office**
507 North Sam Houston
Parkway East, Suite 400
Houston, TX 77060
281-591-2438

**OSHA, Houston South
Area Office**
17625 El Camino Real,
Suite 400
Houston, TX 77058
281-286-0583

OSHA, Lubbock Area Office
Federal Office Building
1205 Texas Avenue,
Room 806
Lubbock, TX 79401
806-472-7681

**OSHA, San Antonio
District Office**
800 Dolorosa Street,
Suite 203
San Antonio, TX 78207
210-472-5040

UTAH

Utah Labor Commission
ESA Wage & Hour Division,
Salt Lake City District Office
160 East 300 South, Suite 300
Salt Lake City, UT 84111
801-530-6800
http://laborcommission.utah.
gov/AntidiscriminationandLabor/
index.html

OSHA, Regional Office
(Region 8)
1999 Broadway, Suite 1690
Denver, CO 80202
720-264-6550

Utah Occupational Safety and
Health Administration
(Federal)
1391 Speer Boulevard,
Suite 210
Denver, CO 80204
303-844-5285

Utah Occupational Safety and
Health Division
(State)
160 East 300 South
Salt Lake City, UT 84114
801-530-6901

ESA Wage & Hour Division,
Salt Lake City District Office
10 East South Temple,
Suite 1680
Salt Lake City, UT 84133
801-524-5706

ESA Wage & Hour Division,
Salt Lake City District Office
150 East Social Hall Avenue,
Suite 695
Salt Lake City, UT 84111
801-524-5706

VERMONT

Vermont Department of Labor
5 Green Mountain Drive
Montpelier, VT 05601
802-828-4000
www.state.vt.us/labind/
wagehr.htm

**OSHA, Regional Office
(Region 1)**
JFK Federal Building,
Room E340
Boston, MA 02203
617-565-9860

**ESA Wage & Hour Division,
Manchester, NH District Office**
1750 Elm Street, Suite 111
Manchester, NH 03104
603-666-7716

VIRGINIA

**Virginia Department of Labor
and Industry**
Labor & Employment Program
Powers-Taylor Building
13 South Thirteenth Street
Richmond, VA 23219
804-371-2327
www.doli.state.va.us

**ESA Wage & Hour Division,
Baltimore, MD District Office**
(Serves Northern Virginia)
Appraisers Stores Building
103 South Gay Street, Room 207

Baltimore, MD 21202
410-962-6211

**ESA Wage & Hour Division,
Charleston, WV Area Office**
(Serves Southwestern Virginia)
500 Quarrier Street, Suite 120
Charleston, WV 25301
304-347-5206

**ESA Wage & Hour Division,
Richmond District Office**
Federal Building, Room 416
400 North 8th Street

Richmond, VA 23219
804-771-2995

OSHA, Regional Office
(Region 3)
The Curtis Center,
Suite 740 West
170 South Independence Mall
West
Philadelphia, PA 19106
215-861-4900

OSHA, Norfolk Area Office
Federal Office Building,
Room 614
200 Granby Mall
Norfolk, VA 23510
757-441-3820

WASHINGTON

Washington Department of
Labor and Industries
7273 Linderson Way Southwest
Tumwater, WA 98501
360-902-5800
www.lni.wa.gov/default.asp

ESA Wage & Hour Division,
Portland, OR District Office
(Serves Wahkiakum and
Klickitat counties)
620 Southwest Main Street,
Room 423
Portland, OR 97205
503 326 3057

ESA Wage & Hour Division,
Seattle District Office
1111 Third Avenue, Suite 755
Seattle, WA 98101
206-398-8039

OSHA, Regional Office
(Region 10)
1111 Third Avenue, Suite 715
Seattle, WA 98101
206-553-5930

OSHA, Bellevue Area Office
505 106th Avenue Northeast,
Suite 302
Bellevue, WA 98004
425-450-5480

WASHINGTON, DC

Department of Employment Services
609 H Street, NE
Washington, DC 20002
202-724-7000
http://does.dc.gov/does/site/default.asp

ESA Wage & Hour Division, Baltimore, MD District Office
Appraisers Stores Building
103 South Gay Street, Room 207
Baltimore, MD 21202
410-962-6211

OSHA, Regional Office (Region 3)
The Curtis Center,
Suite 740 West
170 South Independence Mall West
Philadelphia, PA 19106
215-861-4900

OSHA, Baltimore/Washington Area Office
1099 Winterson Road, Suite 140
Linthicum, MD 21090
410-865-2055

WEST VIRGINIA

West Virginia Division of Labor Wage and Hour Section
State Capitol Complex
Building 6, Room B-749
Charleston, WV 25305
304-558-7890
www.wvlabor.org/home.html

ESA Wage & Hour Division, Baltimore, MD District Office
(Serves the Eastern Panhandle)
Appraisers Stores Building
103 South Gay Street,
Room 207
Baltimore, MD 21202
410-962-6211

ESA Wage & Hour Division, Charleston Area Office
500 Quarrier Street, Suite 120
Charleston, WV 25301
304-347-5206

OSHA, Regional Office (Region 3)
The Curtis Center,
Suite 740 West
170 South Independence Mall West
Philadelphia, PA 19106
215-861-4900

OSHA, Charleston Area Office
405 Capitol Street, Suite 407
Charleston, WV 25301
304-347-5937

WISCONSIN

Wisconsin Equal Rights Division
Labor Standards Bureau,
Madison Office
201 East Washington Avenue
Madison, WI 53708
608-266-6860

Labor Standards Bureau,
Milwaukee Office
819 North Sixth Street
Milwaukee, WI 53203
414-227-4384
www.dwd.state.wi.us/er/
labor_standards_bureau

ESA Wage & Hour Division,
Madison District Office
740 Regent Street, Suite 102
Madison, WI 53715
608-441-5221

OSHA, Regional Office
(Region 5)
230 South Dearborn Street,
Room 3244
Chicago, IL 60604
312-353-2220

OSHA, Appleton Area Office
1648 Tri Park Way
Appleton, WI 54914
920-734-4521

OSHA, Eau Claire Area Office
1310 West Clairemont Avenue
Eau Claire, WI 54701
715-832-9019

OSHA, Madison Area Office
4802 East Broadway
Madison, WI 53716
608-441-5388

OSHA, Milwaukee Area Office
Reuss Federal Plaza
310 West Wisconsin Avenue,
Suite 1180
Milwaukee, WI 53203
414-297-3315

WYOMING

U.S. Department of Labor Occupational Safety and Health Administration
1391 Speer Boulevard,
Suite 210
Denver, CO 80204
303-844-5285
http://wydoe.state.wy.us/doe.asp?ID=9

ESA Wage & Hour Division, Salt Lake City, UT District Office
150 East Social Hall Avenue,
Suite 695
Salt Lake City, UT 84111
801-524-5706

OSHA, Regional Office (Region 8)
1999 Broadway, Suite 1690
Denver, CO 80202
720-264-6550

Appendix C UNEMPLOYMENT INFORMATION BY STATE

This appendix contains a list of the state offices that provide unemployment benefits. The list is organized by state name. Even with double- and triple-checking, sometimes a website is closed prior to publication. If the website listed does not work, you can either go to your state's official website—which is usually www. name of the state.gov—or do an Internet search on the state's name plus the word "unemployment."

ALABAMA

Alabama Department of Industrial Relations
649 Monroe Street
Montgomery, AL 36131
866-234-5382
https://dir.alabama.gov/uc/

ALASKA

Alaska Department of Labor and Workforce Development
Employment Security Division
Unemployment Insurance Program
P.O. Box 115509
Juneau, AK 99811
907-465-5552
http://labor.state.ak.us/esd_unemployment_insurance/biff-splash.htm

ARIZONA

Arizona Department of Economic Security
Employment Security Administration
Phoenix Office (for Maricopa County residents only)
P. O. Box 29225
Phoenix, AZ 85038
602-364-2722 (Phoenix)
520-791-2722 (Tucson)
877-600-2722 (other areas)
www.azdes.gov/esa/uibenefits/uibhome.asp

ARKANSAS

Arkansas Department of Workforce Services
#2 Capitol Mall
Little Rock, AR 72201
501-907-2590
www.accessarkansas.org/esd

CALIFORNIA

Employment Development Department
800 Capitol Mall, MIC 83
Sacramento, CA 95814
800-300-5616
www.edd.ca.gov/eddhome.htm

COLORADO

Colorado Department of Labor and Employment
Division of Employment and Training
633 17th Street, Suite 201
Denver, CO 80202
303-318-9000
800-388-5515
www.coworkforce.com

CONNECTICUT

Connecticut Department of Labor
200 Folly Brook Boulevard
Wethersfield, CT 06109
860-263-6000
www.ctdol.state.ct.us/progsupt/unemplt/unemployment.htm

DELAWARE

Delaware Department of Labor
Division of Unemployment Insurance, Dover Office
1114 South Dupont Highway, Suite 103
Dover, DE 19901
302-739-5461

Division of Unemployment Insurance, Georgetown Office
600 North Dupont Highway, Suite 205
Georgetown, DE 19947
302-856-5611

Division of Unemployment Insurance, Newark Office
Pencader Corporate Center
225 Corporate Boulevard, Suite 108
Newark, DE 19702
302-368-6600

Division of Unemployment Insurance, Wilmington Office
4425 North Market Street
Wilmington, DE 19802
302-761-8446
www.delawareworks.com/Unemployment/welcome.shtml

FLORIDA

Florida Agency for Workforce Innovation
107 East Madison Street
Caldwell Building
Tallahassee, FL 32399-4120
850-245-7105
www.floridajobs.org/unemployment

GEORGIA

Georgia Department of Labor
Unemployment Insurance Division
404-56-3045
www.dol.state.ga.us/js/unemployment_benefits_individuals.htm

HAWAII

Hawaii Department of Labor and Industrial Relations
Unemployment Insurance Division
Princess Ruth Keelikolani Building
830 Punchbowl Street
Honolulu, HI 96813
808-643-5555
877-215-5793
www.hawaii.gov/labor

IDAHO

Idaho Department of Labor
317 West Main Street
Boise, ID 83735
208-332-3570
http://labor.idaho.gov/dnn/Default.aspx?alias=labor.idaho.gov/dnn/idl

ILLINOIS

Illinois Department of Employment Security (IDES)
Chicago Office
33 South State Street
Chicago, IL 60603
312-793-5700
www.ides.state.il.us

Illinois Department of Employment Security (IDES)
Springfield Office
850 East Madison Street
Springfield, IL 62702
217-785-5069
www.ides.state.il.us

INDIANA

Indiana Department of Workforce Development
10 North Senate Avenue
Indianapolis, IN 46204
800-891-6499
www.in.gov/dwd

IOWA

Iowa Workforce Development
Unemployment Insurance Services Division
1000 East Grand Avenue
Des Moines, IA 50319
515-281-5387
www.iowaworkforce.org/ui/index.html

KANSAS

Kansas Unemployment Insurance Service
P.O. Box 3539
Topeka, KS 66601
785-575-1460
800-292-6333
www.hr.state.ks.us/home-html/subpage2.htm

KENTUCKY

Department for Employment Services
Unemployment Insurance
275 East Main Street
Frankfort, KY 40621
502-564-2900
www.des.ky.gov/des/ui/ui.asp

LOUISIANA

Louisiana Department of Labor
Office of Regulatory Services
1001 North 23rd Street
Baton Rouge, LA 70802
225-342-3111
www.laworks.net/UnemploymentInsurance/UI_MainMenu.asp

MAINE

Maine Department of Labor
Bureau of Unemployment Compensation
45 Commerce Drive
Augusta, ME 04333
207-287-2316
www.state.me.us/labor/uibennys/index.html

MARYLAND

Maryland Division of Labor and Industry
Office of Unemployment Insurance
1100 North Eutaw Street
Baltimore, MD 21201
410-949-0022 (Baltimore area/out of state)
800-827-4839 (rest of Maryland)
www.dllr.state.md.us/employment/unemployment.html

MASSACHUSETTS

Massachusetts Department of Employment & Training
Charles F. Hurley Building
19 Staniford Street
Boston, MA 02114
617-626-6560
www.detma.org/DETUI.htm

MICHIGAN

Michigan Department of Consumer and Industry Services
Bureau of Workers' and Unemployment Compensation
3024 West Grand Boulevard, Suite 11-500
Detroit, MI 48202
800-638-3995
www.michigan.gov/uia

MINNESOTA

Minnesota Department of Economic Security
P.O. Box 75576
St. Paul, MN 55175
651-296-3745
www.uinm.org

MISSISSIPPI

Mississippi Department of Employment Security
1235 Echelon Parkway
P.O. Box 1699
Jackson, MS 39215
601-321-60000
www.mdes.ms.gov/wps/portal

MISSOURI

Missouri Division of Labor and Industrial Relations
421 East Dunklin Street
P.O. Box 504
Jefferson City, MO 65102
573-751-3215
www.ui.dolir.mo.gov/som

MONTANA

Montana Department of Labor and Industry
Unemployment Insurance Division
P.O. Box 8020
Helena, MT 59604
406-444-2545
http://uid.dli.mt.gov/

NEBRASKA

Nebraska Department of Labor
Unemployment Insurance Program, Lincoln Claims Center
P. O. Box 95200
Lincoln, NE 68501
402-458-2500

Unemployment Insurance Program, Omaha Claims Center
P. O. Box 642330
Omaha, NE 68164
402-829-2800, Option 5
www.dol.state.ne.us/nwd/center.cfm?PRICAT=1&SUBCAT=1B

NEVADA

Nevada Department of Employment, Training and Rehabilitation
Employment Security Division
500 East Third Street
Carson City, NV 89713
775-684-0350 (Northern Nevada)
702-486-0350 (Southern Nevada)
888-890-8211 (Rural Nevada)
www.detr.state.nv.us/uiben/uiben_uiben.htm

NEW HAMPSHIRE

New Hampshire Department of Employment Security
32 South Main Street
Concord, NH 03301
603-224-3311
800-852-3400
www.nh.gov/nhes

NEW JERSEY

New Jersey Department of Labor and Workforce Development
Division of Unemployment Insurance
P.O. Box 058
Trenton, NJ 08625
609-292-7162
http://lwd.dol.state.nj.us/labor/ui/ui_index.html

NEW MEXICO

New Mexico Department of Labor
Unemployment Insurance Bureau, Employment Security Division
401 Broadway Northeast
Albuquerque, NM 87102
505-841-2000
www.dol.state.nm.us/dol_esd.html

NEW YORK

New York State Department of Labor
Unemployment Insurance Program
State Office Building Campus, Room 500
Albany, NY 12240
888-209-8124
www.labor.state.ny.us/ui/ui_index.shtm

NORTH CAROLINA

Employment Security Commission of North Carolina
700 Wade Avenue
Raleigh, NC 27605
919-733-4329
www.ncesc.com

NORTH DAKOTA

Job Service North Dakota
P.O. Box 5507
Bismarck, ND 58506-5507
701-328-2825
800-732-9787
www.jobsnd.com

OHIO

Ohio Department of Job & Family Services
Office of Unemployment Compensation
30 East Broad Street, 32nd Floor
Columbus, OH 43215
877-644-6562
http://unemployment.ohio.gov

OKLAHOMA

Oklahoma Employment Security Commission
Will Rogers Memorial Office Building
2401 North Lincoln Boulevard
Oklahoma City, OK 73105
405-557-0200
www.oesc.state.ok.us

OREGON

Oregon Employment Department
www.oregon.gov/EMPLOY/UI/index.shtml

PENNSYLVANIA

Pennsylvania Department of Labor and Industry
Unemployment Compensation Claims Information Center
6th Floor, Labor & Industry Bldg.
Seventh & Forster Streets
Harrisburg, PA 17121
888-313-7284
www.dli.state.pa.us/landi/cwp/view.asp?a=202&Q=67546&landiR
NavradC6865=l

RHODE ISLAND

Rhode Island Department of Labor & Training
Unemployment Insurance
Center General Complex
1511 Pontiac Avenue
Cranston, RI 02920
401-243-9100
www.dlt.ri.gov/ui

SOUTH CAROLINA

South Carolina Employment Security Commission
P. O. Box 995
1550 Gadsden St.
Columbia, SC 29202
803-737-3071
www.sces.org

SOUTH DAKOTA

South Dakota Department of Labor
Unemployment Insurance
420 South Roosevelt Street
P.O. Box 4730
Aberdeen, SD 57402
605-626-2452
http://dol.sd.gov/ui/default.aspx

TENNESSEE

Tennessee Department of Labor and Workforce Development
Division of Employment Security
UI Claims Center
P.O. Box 280870
Nashville, TN 37228
615-253-0800, 877-813-0950
www.state.tn.us/labor-wfd/esdiv.html

TEXAS

Texas Workforce Commission
101 East 15th Street,
Austin, TX 78778
800-939-6631
www.twc.state.tx.us

UTAH

Utah Department of Workforce Services
Unemployment Compensation
P.O. Box 45249
Salt Lake City, UT 84145
801-526-9675
http://jobs.utah.gov/ui/

VERMONT

Vermont Department of Employment and Training
Unemployment Compensation Division
5 Green Mountain Drive
P.O. Box 488
Montpelier, VT 05601
877-214-3330
http://labor.vermont.gov/

VIRGINIA

Virginia Employment Commission
Richmond Central Office
703 East Main Street
Richmond, VA 23219
804-786-1485
www.vec.state.va.us/index_ui.cfm?loc=unins&info=insur

WASHINGTON

Washington Employment Security Department
Unemployment Insurance, King County Center
P.O. Box 47076
Seattle, WA 98146
206-766-6000 (English)
206-766-6063 (Spanish)
800-362-4636 (English)
800-360-2271 (Spanish)

Unemployment Insurance, Spokane Center
P.O. Box 14857
Spokane, WA 99214
509-893-7000 (English)
509-893-7063 (Spanish)
800-362-4636 (English)
800-360-2271 (Spanish)
www.wa.gov/esd/ui.htm

WASHINGTON, DC

DC Department of Employment Services
Government of the District of Columbia
64 New York Avenue NE, Suite 3000
Washington, DC 20002
202-724-7000
http://does.ci.washington.dc.us/services/unemployment.shtm

WEST VIRGINIA

West Virginia Bureau of Employment Programs
Unemployment Compensation Division
1321 Plaza East
Charleston, WV 25330
304-558-2624
www.wvbep.org/bep/uc

WISCONSIN

Wisconsin Department of Workforce Development
Unemployment Insurance Division
Madison: 608-232-0678 (claims filing); 608-232-0824
(questions/assistance)
Milwaukee: 414-438-7700 (claims filing); 414-438-7713
(questions/assistance)
Elsewhere: 800-822-5246 (claims filing); 800-494-4944
(questions/assistance)
www.dwd.state.wi.us/ui

WYOMING

Wyoming Department of Employment
Unemployment Insurance Division
100 West Midwest
P.O. Box 2760
Casper, WY 82602
307-235-3253
http://wydoe.state.wy.us/doe.asp?ID=11

WORKERS' COMPENSATION PROGRAMS BY STATE

This appendix contains a list of the state offices that provide information on filing workers' compensation claims. The list is organized by state name. Even with double- and triple-checking, sometimes a website is closed prior to publication. If the website listed does not work, you can either go to your state's official website—which is usually www.name of the state.gov—or do an Internet search on the state's name plus the words "workers' compensation."

ALABAMA

Alabama Department of Industrial Relations
649 Monroe Street
Montgomery, AL 36131
800-923-2533
http://dir.alabama.gov/wc/

ALASKA

Alaska Department of Labor
Workers' Compensation Division
P.O. Box 115512
Juneau, AK 99811
907-465-2790
http://labor.state.ak.us/wc/home.htm

ARIZONA

Industrial Commission of Arizona
Claims Division
800 West Washington Street
P.O. Box 19070
Phoenix, AZ 85007
602-542-4661
www.ica.state.az.us/workersCompensation/index.html

ARKANSAS

Arkansas Workers' Compensation Commission
324 Spring Street
P. O. Box 950
Little Rock, AR 72203
501-682-3930
800-622-4472
www.awcc.state.ar.us

CALIFORNIA

Division of Workers' Compensation
455 Golden Gate Ave., 9th Floor
San Francisco, CA 94102
415-703-4600
866-924-9757
www.dir.ca.gov/dwc

COLORADO

Colorado Department of Labor & Employment
Division of Workers' Compensation
633 17th Street, Suite 400
Denver, CO 80202
303-575-8700
888-390-7936
www.coworkforce.com/dwc

CONNECTICUT

Connecticut Workers' Compensation Commission
21 Oak Street
Hartford, CT 06106
860-493-1500
800-223-9675
http://wcc.state.ct.us/index.html

DELAWARE

Delaware Department of Labor, Division of Industrial Affairs
Office of Workers' Compensation
Newark Office
225 Corporate Boulevard, Suite 104
Newark, DE 19702

Delaware Department of Labor, Division of Industrial Affairs
Office of Workers' Compensation
Milford Office
24 Northwest Front Street, Suite 100
Milford, DE 19963
302-422-1392

Delaware Department of Labor, Division of Industrial Affairs
Office of Workers' Compensation
Wilmington Office
4425 North Market Street, 3rd Floor
Wilmington, DE 19802
302-761-8200
www.delawareworks.com/industrialaffairs/services/workerscomp.shtml

FLORIDA
Division of Workers' Compensation
Employee Assistance Office
200 East Gaines Street
Tallahassee, FL 32399-4225
850-921-6966, 800-342-1741
www.fldfs.com/WC

GEORGIA
Georgia Board of Workers' Compensation
270 Peachtree Street, NW
Atlanta, GA 30303
404-656-3875
800-533-0682
www.ganet.org/sbwc

HAWAII
Hawaii Department of Labor and Industrial Relations
Disability Compensation Division
830 Punchbowl Street, Room 211
P. O. Box 3769
Honolulu, HI 96813
808-586-8842
http://hawaii.gov/labor

IDAHO

Idaho Industrial Commission
Statehouse Mail
317 Main Street
P. O. Box 83720
Boise, ID 83720
208-334-6000
800-950-2110
www.iic.idaho.gov

ILLINOIS

Illinois Industrial Commission
100 West Randolph Street, Suite 8-200
Chicago, IL 60601
312-814-6611
866-352-3033
www.state.il.us/agency/iic

INDIANA

Workers' Compensation Board of Indiana
402 West Washington Street, Room W-196
Indianapolis, IN 46204
317-232-3808
www.in.gov/workcomp

IOWA

Iowa Workforce Development
Division of Workers' Compensation
1000 East Grand Avenue
Des Moines, Iowa 50319
515-281-5387

800-JOB-IOWA
www.iowaworkforce.org/wc/index.html

KANSAS
Kansas Department of Human Resources
Division of Workers' Compensation
401 Southwest Topeka Boulevard
Topeka, KS 66603
785-296-3441
800-322-0353
www.dol.ks.gov/WC/html/wc_ALL.html

KENTUCKY
Kentucky Labor Cabinet
Department of Workers' Claims
Prevention Park
657 Chamberlain Avenue
Frankfort, KY 40601
502-564-5550
800-554-8601
www.labor.ky.gov/workersclaims

LOUISIANA
Louisiana Department of Labor
Office of Workers' Compensation Administration
1001 North 23rd Street
P. O. Box 94040
Baton Rouge, LA 70802
225-342-7555
800-756-7123
www.laworks.net/WorkersComp/OWC_MainMenu.asp

MAINE

Maine Workers' Compensation Board
27 State House Station
Augusta, ME 04333
207-287-3751
888-801-9087
www.state.me.us/wcb

MARYLAND

Maryland Workers' Compensation Commission
10 East Baltimore Street
Baltimore, MD 21202
410-864-5100
800-492-0479
www.wcc.state.md.us

MASSACHUSETTS

Massachusetts Department of Industrial Accidents
600 Washington Street, 7th Floor
Boston, MA 02111
617-727-4900
800-323-3249
www.state.ma.us/dia/index.htm

MICHIGAN

Bureau of Workers' Disability Compensation
7150 Harris Drive
Dimondale, MI 48821
888-396-5041
www.michigan.gov/wca

MINNESOTA

Minnesota Department of Labor and Industry
Workers' Compensation Agency
443 Lafayette Road North
St. Paul, MN 55155
651-284-5018
800-342-5354
www.doli.state.mn.us/workcomp.html

MISSISSIPPI

Mississippi Workers' Compensation Commission
1428 Lakeland Drive
Jackson, MS 39216
601-987-4200
866-473-6992
www.mwcc.state.ms.us

MISSOURI

Missouri Department of Labor and Industrial Relations
Division of Workers' Compensation
3315 West Truman Boulevard, Room 131
P.O. Box 58
Jefferson City, MO 65102
573-751-4231
800-775-2667
www.mouitax.com/wc/index.asp

MONTANA

Montana Department of Labor and Industry
Employment Relations Division
Workers' Compensation Claims Assistance Bureau

1805 Prospect Avenue
P. O. Box 8011
Helena, MT 59624
406-444-6543
800-772-2141
http://erd.dli.mt.gov/wcregs/wcrhome.asp

NEBRASKA

Nebraska Workers' Compensation Court
Capitol Building
P. O. Box 98908
Lincoln, NE 68509
402-471-6468
800-599-5155
www.nol.org/workcomp

NEVADA

Nevada Division of Industrial Relations
Workers' Compensation Section, Northern District
400 West King Street, Suite 400
Carson City, NV 89703
775-684-7270

Nevada Division of Industrial Relations
Workers' Compensation Section, Southern District
1301 North Green Valley Parkway, Suite 200
Henderson, NV 89074
702-486-9080
http://dirweb.state.nv.us/WCS/wcs.htm

NEW HAMPSHIRE

New Hampshire Department of Labor
Workers' Compensation Division
95 Pleasant Street
Concord, NH 03301
603-271-3174
800-272-4353
www.labor.state.nh.us/injured_worker.asp

NEW JERSEY

New Jersey Department of Labor
Division of Workers' Compensation
John Fitch Plaza
P.O. Box 381
Trenton, NJ 08625
609-292-2515
http://lwd.dol.state.nj.us/labor/wc/wc_index.html

NEW MEXICO

Workers' Compensation Administration
2410 Centre Avenue SE
P. O. Box 27198
Albuquerque, NM 87125
505-841-6000
800-255-7965
www.state.nm.us/wca

NEW YORK

New York Workers' Compensation Board
20 Park Street
Albany, NY 12207
518-474-6670

877-632-4996
www.wcb.state.ny.us

NORTH CAROLINA

North Carolina Industrial Commission
4319 Mail Service Center
Raleigh, NC 27699
919-807-2500
800-688-8349
www.comp.state.nc.us

NORTH DAKOTA

North Dakota Workers' Compensation
1600 East Century Avenue, Suite 1
Bismarck, ND 58503
701-328-3800
800-777-5033
www.workforcesafety.com

OHIO

Ohio Bureau of Workers' Compensation
30 West Spring Street
Columbus, OH 43215
800-644-6292
www.ohiobwc.com

OKLAHOMA

Oklahoma Workers' Compensation Court
1915 North Stiles Avenue
Oklahoma City, OK 73105
405-522-8600

800-522-8210
www.owcc.state.ok.us

OREGON

Oregon Workers' Compensation Division
350 Winter Street, NE
P.O. Box 14480
Salem, OR 97309
503-947-7810
800-452-0288
www.cbs.state.or.us/wcd

PENNSYLVANIA

Pennsylvania Department of Labor and Industry
Bureau of Workers' Compensation
1171 South Cameron Street, Room 324
Harrisburg, PA 17104
717-783-5421
800-482-2383
www.dli.state.pa.us/landi/cwp/view.asp?a=138&q=220671

RHODE ISLAND

Rhode Island Department of Labor and Training
Division of Workers' Compensation
1511 Pontiac Avenue, Building 69, Second Floor
P. O. Box 20190
Cranston, RI 02920
401-462-8100
401-462-8125
www.dlt.ri.gov/wc

SOUTH CAROLINA

South Carolina Workers' Compensation Commission
1612 Marion Street
P. O. Box 1715
Columbia, SC 29201
803-737-5700
800-868-4244
www.wcc.state.sc.us

SOUTH DAKOTA

South Dakota Department of Labor
Division of Labor & Management
Kneip Building
700 Governors Drive
Pierre, SD 57501
605-773-3681
http://dol.sd.gov/workerscomp/default.aspx

TENNESSEE

Tennessee Department of Labor & Workforce Development
Division of Workers' Compensation
220 French Landing Drive
Nashville, TN 37243
615-532-4812
800-332-2667
www.state.tn.us/labor-wfd/wcomp.html

TEXAS

Texas Division of Workers' Compensation
Southfield Building, MS-4C
4000 South IH-35

Austin, TX 78704
512-804-4000
800-252-7031www.tdi.state.tx.us/wc/indexwc.html

UTAH

Labor Commission of Utah
Division of Industrial Accidents
160 East 300 South, 3rd Floor
P. O. Box 146610
Salt Lake City, UT 84114
801-530-6800
800-530-5090
http://laborcommission.utah.gov/IndustrialAccidents/index.html

VERMONT

Vermont Department of Labor and Industry
Workers' Compensation Division
5 Green Mountain Drive
P.O. Box 488
Montpelier, VT 05601
802-828-2286
www.state.vt.us/labind/wcindex.htm

VIRGINIA

Virginia Workers' Compensation Commission
1000 DMV Drive
Richmond, VA 23220
804-367-8600
877-664-2566
www.vwc.state.va.us

WASHINGTON

Washington Department of Labor and Industries
Industrial Insurance Services Division
7273 Linderson Way, SW
Tumwater, WA 98501
360-902-5800
800-547-8367
www.lni.wa.gov/ClaimsIns/Claims/default.asp

WASHINGTON, DC

DC Department of Employment Services
Labor Standards Bureau
Office of Workers' Compensation
64 New York Avenue, NE, 2nd floor
Washington, DC 20002
202-671-1000
http://does.dc.gov/does/cwp/view,a,1232,q,537428.asp

WEST VIRGINIA

West Virginia Bureau of Employment Programs
Workers' Compensation Division
4700 MacCorkle Avenue, SE
Charleston, WV 25304
304-926-5048
800-628-4265
www.wvwcc.org

WISCONSIN

Department of Workforce Development
Workers' Compensation Division
201 East Washington Avenue, Room C-100
P. O. Box 7901
Madison, WI 53707
608-266-1340
www.dwd.state.wi.us/wc

WYOMING

Wyoming Department of Employment
Workers' Safety and Compensation Division
1510 East Pershing Boulevard
Cheyenne, WY 82002
307-777-7441
http://wydoe.state.wy.us/doe.asp?ID=9

INTERNET RESOURCES

BULLIES IN THE WORKPLACE

Workplace Bullying Institute
www.bullyfreeworkplace.org
www.bullyinginstitute.org

Healthy Workplace Advocates, Maryland
www.mdstopbully.com

Healthy Workplace Advocates, New York
www.nyhwa.org

Healthy Workplace Advocates, Vermont
www.vtbullybusters.org

COBRA

www.dol.gov/ebsa/faqs/faq_consumer_cobra.HTML

DEPARTMENT OF LABOR

www.dol.gov

<u>EMPLOYMENT ATTORNEYS</u>
The National Employment Lawyers Association
www.nela.org

Martindale Hubbard attorney listings
www.martindale.com

Findlaw
www.findlaw.com

Find Great Lawyers
www.findgreatlawyers.com

<u>EQUAL EMPLOYMENT OPPORTUNITY COMMISSION (EEOC)</u>
www.eeoc.gov

Find office near you
www.eeoc.gov/offices.html

Information on caregiver status
www.worklifelaw.org

www.eeoc.gov/policy/docs/caregiving.html

GOVERNMENT EMPLOYEES

Merit Systems Protection Board (MSPB)

www.mspb.gov

Office of Personnel Management (OPM)

www.opm.gov

OPM on sexual orientation

www.opm.gov/er/address2/guide01.htm.

Office of Special Counsel (OSC)

www.osc.gov/ppp.htm

GOVERNMENT WEBSITES, BY AGENCY

www.firstgov.gov

NATIONAL LABOR RELATIONS BOARD (NLRB)

www.nlrb.gov

OCCUPATIONAL SAFETY AND HEALTHY ADMINISTRATION (OSHA)

www.osha.gov

VETERANS

www.dol.gov/vets

OPM's *Veterans Guide*
www.opm.gov/veterans/html/vetguide.asp

OPM's Disabled Veterans Affirmative Action Program
www.opm.gov/veterans/dvaap.asp

Index

About the Author

Diana Brodman Summers received her law degree from DePaul University College of Law in Chicago. She is an arbitrator for both the Cook and DuPage county mandatory arbitration programs. She currently maintains a law practice near Chicago.